The Logistics Audit

Extraordinary technological progress, but also the experience gained from the global COVID-19 pandemic, force the future vision of the world's economic development to assume a close coexistence and intense interaction between production (manufacturing) and logistics and supply-chain management. This perspective requires that the current functioning of organizations will have to be radically remodeled so that they can face not only market competition but also the turbulent changes (volatility, uncertainty, complexity, and ambiguity - VUCA) that take place in their close environment. Therefore, in the next few years, one of the most important tools for improving organizations may become industry audits, especially the logistics audit.

This book explores the development, methods, and impact of logistics audits on organizations. In a holistic way, the book refers to topics such as internal audit, control, logistics system of enterprises, principles of conducting logistics audit and its problem areas (risk), logistics audit of procurement, production, warehousing, distribution, and supply chains, impact of the digital economy on organizations, and the European market for logistics audit services. Undoubtedly, the greatest asset of this book is that, in international terms, it is the first compact book devoted to the issue of logistics audit.

Unique and timely, the book will be an essential resource for academics and postgraduate students of logistics supply-chain management, and global operations in particular.

Piotr Buła is an Associate Professor and Head of the International Management Department at Krakow University of Economics (KUE), Poland, Vice-Rector for Projects and Cooperation (KUE), former Director of Cracow School of Business (CUE), Senior Research Professor in Business Management Department at the University of Johannesburg, South Africa, and Grand Valley State University scholarship holder. He is the author or co-author of more than 175 publications in economics and management. His research interests focus on aspects related to the application of artificial intelligence and neuromanagement, risk management, internal audit, international management, and logistics. A member of international organizations associating professors and business practitioners in the management area: EFMD, CEEMAN, IMDA, CBATA, EIBA, GSSI, IAMB, EECSA, SAIMS.

Bartosz Niedzielski is an Assistant Professor at Krakow University of Economics, Poland. He studied and conducted scientific activities, among other subjects, at the University of Greenwich (UK), University of Oxford (UK), London School of Economics (UK), Deggendorf Institute of Technology (DE), and Jagiellonian University (PL). He has over ten years of professional experience gained in global corporations in the BPO/SCC sector (mainly at HSBC). His research interests focus on aspects related to the application of artificial intelligence in organizations, management, and internal audit. He is the author or co-author of more than 50 scientific publications in economics and management, including the monograph entitled *Management, Organizations and Artificial Intelligence: Where Theory Meets Practice* (Routledge, 2021).

Routledge Focus on Business and Management

The fields of business and management have grown exponentially as areas of research and education. This growth presents challenges for readers trying to keep up with the latest important insights. *Routledge Focus on Business and Management* presents small books on big topics and how they intersect with the world of business research.

Individually, each title in the series provides coverage of a key academic topic, whilst collectively, the series forms a comprehensive collection across the business disciplines.

Systems Thinking and Sustainable Healthcare Delivery
Ben Fong

Gender Diversity and Inclusion at Work
Divergent Views from Turkey
Zeynep Özsoy, Mustafa Şenyücel and Beyza Oba

Management and Visualisation
Seeing Beyond the Strategic
Gordon Fletcher

Knowledge Management and AI in Society 5.0
Manlio Del Giudice, Veronica Scuotto and Armando Papa

The Logistics Audit
Methods, Organization, and Practice
Piotr Buła and Bartosz Niedzielski

For more information about this series, please visit: www.routledge.com/
Routledge-Focus-on-Business-and-Management/book-series/FBM

The Logistics Audit
Methods, Organization, and Practice

Piotr Buła and Bartosz Niedzielski

Routledge
Taylor & Francis Group

LONDON AND NEW YORK

First published 2023
by Routledge
4 Park Square, Milton Park, Abingdon, Oxon OX14 4RN

and by Routledge
605 Third Avenue, New York, NY 10158

Routledge is an imprint of the Taylor & Francis Group, an informa business

© 2023 Piotr Buła and Bartosz Niedzielski

The right of Piotr Buła and Bartosz Niedzielski to be identified as authors of this work has been asserted in accordance with sections 77 and 78 of the Copyright, Designs and Patents Act 1988.

British Library Cataloguing-in-Publication Data
A catalogue record for this book is available from the British Library

ISBN: 978-1-032-46126-7 (hbk)
ISBN: 978-1-032-46127-4 (pbk)
ISBN: 978-1-003-38018-4 (ebk)

DOI: 10.4324/9781003380184

Typeset in Times New Roman
by Deanta Global Publishing Services, Chennai, India

Contents

Acknowledgments

We had no doubt that attempting to integrate the knowledge of audit and logistics scattered throughout the literature would be both a demanding and an inspiring endeavor. The biggest challenge was the fact that both subdisciplines of management and quality sciences draw on a number of other academic specialties, notably economics, finance, and praxeology. The limitations adopted in the course of research allowed us to focus primarily on logistics audit as a comprehensive technique and independent diagnostic tool of company logistics systems.

In doing so, we have set a new research direction that may prove useful for future explorations in logistics audit and all its components, from procurement to distribution – a fact that was also noted by the book's reviewers, for which we are extremely grateful. With this in mind, we, as authors, believe that the book has met or will meet its objectives, which include, first and foremost, an attempt to organize and supplement existing knowledge on logistics audit in the broader context of other types of audit and, secondly, to prepare a compact publication that will provide a wide audience with a basic reference on logistics audit and related topics.

We would like to take this opportunity to express our gratitude to all the wonderful people we met while researching and writing the book, people who made it possible. First, we would like to thank the students of International Logistics at our university, who were the moving spirit behind the entire undertaking. It was their enthusiasm and willingness to deepen their knowledge and improve their skills that started us working. We would also like to express our thanks to the authorities of the Krakow University of Economics, whose organizational and financial support turned out to be necessary almost at every stage of the implementation of this project. We are especially grateful to Anna Chrabąszcz, who acted as the managing editor and coordinator of the publishing process. Her commitment, efficiency, and editorial conscientiousness will remain in our grateful memory for a long time. It is impossible not to mention Alex Atkinson and her team at

Routledge, whose professionalism, to quote Kevin Powers, "was character-ised by a certain evolutionary beauty." The authors would also like to thank the anonymous reviewers for their time and effort, which will always be an important element of science. Finally, special thanks go to our loved ones, who have been with us at every stage of the writing process and who often understand us better than we understand ourselves.

Piotr Buła and Bartosz Niedzielski

Introduction

Today, as never before, organizations must constantly evolve and quickly adapt to the changing environment around them. This situation requires them to regularly face several challenges, whose level of intensity varies and is the result of both the external and internal environment of the organization. Most often these challenges concern aspects related to business, legal, regulatory, technological requirements, or – increasingly often – security, which, due to the rapidly growing number and size of cyberattacks in the world,[1] has now become more important than freedom itself. Nevertheless, what most determines the compulsion to change the current way of functioning of the organization and its business model are technological megatrends. In practice, they reshape reality in the economic, social, legal, and political dimensions of every contemporary organization. And although the power of influence that global technological trends have on the economies of many countries may vary, it is experienced to a greater or lesser extent by practically everyone. Technological novelties in the form of artificial intelligence, blockchain, drones, Internet of Things, robots, and virtual reality reach both poor and rich countries, large and small organizations, developed and underdeveloped nations, less and more educated societies, all religions, and both America and Africa. Thanks to these circumstances, the flat world theory, formulated by Thomas Friedman at the dawn of the 21st century, is gaining in importance and at the same time underscores that the limitations, barriers, and boundaries for innovative technologies are not confirmed – in the physical sense – in the reality that surrounds us.

Considering the above, it is impossible not to notice that the permanent turbulence of the environment generates constant pressure on the management of the organization, especially in relation to the need to achieve the strategic goals set before it. However, when taking into account the dynamics of globalization processes, the intensification of competition activities, the growing importance of risk and uncertainty in the world, as well as

DOI: 10.4324/9781003380184-1

the forces driving the development of digitization, the achievement of such goals will not be possible without the organization having specific knowledge, experience, meta-skills, qualified specialists, and tools. All of these elements must evolve on par with the changing environment so that they can productively serve the leadership in managing the entire organization. An important role in this process will probably be played by internal audits in general, and industry audits in particular. These are tools whose inherent feature is to help organizations achieve their fundamental goals. And because data, technology, and management tools are currently intertwined in almost every aspect of the functioning of the organization, this situation will also force the audit to change its current form and mode of implementation. To put it simply, there will be a transition – most likely within the next decade – from a fourth-generation audit to a fifth-generation one, which will be performed more often than before in remote form and using digital technologies. This probability entitles us to put forward the thesis that audits of the future will be digital audits. But, due to the current challenges faced by organizations, including the dynamic development of the digital economy or the still unflagging popularity of logistics – exemplified by the flourishing of the logistics services market in Poland, Europe, and beyond – a deeper look at management aspects is also needed, in the context of the logistics audit itself. Its development, as an industry audit, took place at the beginning of the 1990s, while the increase in popularity fell at the beginning of the 21st century. This makes the logistics audit, as a comprehensive and independent tool for assessing the company's logistics system, a relatively young concept, in contrast to the history of audit itself, which is over 70 years old. Consequently, management science literature – apart from definitional approaches – has not seen any wider studies and publications (including books or scientific monographs) that would satisfactorily deal with the essence, scope, and complexity of this issue. This applies to publications in English, Polish, and other languages. In addition, logistic audit terms formulated mostly in articles and industry reports, have often been and still are built using vague terms, which in practice leads to the generation of an excessive number of definitions of this concept in the scientific and journalistic literature, and consequently to terminological chaos. What's more, it is also worth noting that the elements, threads, thoughts, or problems discussed in the literature regarding the logistics audit often remain without verification or evaluation regarding the degree of their impact on management theories. Meanwhile, and this should not be forgotten, progress in science is possible thanks to the critical juxtaposing of observed things with the current state of knowledge, including strictly theoretical knowledge. It is therefore possible to identify in management sciences the existence of a certain gap in the issues devoted to the logistics audit, and, through this book, an attempt was made to create a publication whose content, layout, and richness of the presented approaches contribute to the implementation of three basic goals. First, the book is an attempt to organize, supplement, and enrich the existing knowledge about the logistics audit, compared to other types of audit. Second, it is to serve as a basic source of knowledge for a wide range of recipients interested in the subject of logistics audit, including students of higher education institutions, specialists, practitioners, academic teachers, middle and senior managers, and other people who want to deepen their knowledge in this field. And third, it is intended to be a source of inspiration for scientists and researchers who will want to conduct scientific research on the theoretical and practical aspects of the development of logistics audit in organizations and in management sciences.

The book is structured around four chapters.

Chapter 1 discusses the issues of general audit, taking into account its etymological and historical perspective. An audit typology is presented along with the goals and mission it has to achieve in the context of the organization. Then, in tabular terms, the similarities and differences between external and internal audits are presented. Similar *differentia specifica* are also presented in relation to internal audit and control, due to the frequent occurrence of blurred – also in the literature – boundaries between audit and controlling. The chapter ends with a description of tasks, work standards, and the role played by the auditor in the organization from the point of view of audit implementation. In addition, the chapter is enriched with the presentation – in tabular terms – of the scope of activities performed by the auditor and his competences.

Chapter 2 is almost entirely devoted to the logistic audit methodology. At the beginning, the logistics system of the company is described in a holistic manner, taking into account the divisions to which it is subject in the literature on the topic. Next, the basic objectives of the logistics audit are presented, including the processes and problem areas that may be its subject. These explanations are firmly embedded in the context of considerations regarding the so-called industry audits, which in practice – but also in science – are perceived as important sources of information on the condition of a given unit. In addition, an important part of this chapter is the description of the basic stages of logistics audit implementation, which are also presented in tabular form, while the procedure for its conduct is presented in graphical form. The final part of the chapter concerns the impact of the Fourth Industrial Revolution (Industry 4.0) on the changes taking place in auditing, especially in relation to the goals set for it, the style of implementation of audit tasks, the set of tools and technologies used, and the identification of places related to the accumulation of the greatest risk.

Chapter 3 presents a modular approach to logistics auditing, presenting the most well-known types, divided into: logistics audit of procurement, logistics audit of production, logistics audit of the warehouse, logistics audit of distribution, and, lastly, logistics audit of the supply chain.

Chapter 4 is more managerial in nature and focuses on two basic aspects. Firstly, it presents tools (indicators) that in practice can be used to analyze the potential of the company's logistics system and defines the risks occurring in the logistics system of the organization. Secondly, it presents a brief analysis of the development of the logistics audit services market in the national dimension, also in relation to the changes that are taking place in the market in the context of the progressing phenomenon of digitization.

Each of the chapters ends with a set of prepared control and analytical questions, whose task is to verify knowledge about the issues raised and stimulate readers to intellectual effort related to critical thinking, the final "product" of which will be the evaluation of the content read.

At the end of this introduction, the authors express the hope that the book will meet the expectations that are placed on it. To a large extent, they concern the fact that, for each of the readers, it becomes a useful item in deepening knowledge about management in general and logistics auditing in particular. May the lesson of this book be a source of development of their own talents and interests for all.

Piotr Buła and Bartosz Niedzielski

Note

1 As an example, it is worth quoting events that occurred only in the first half of 2020. The first of them was associated with the loss of USD 2.3 million by Manor Independent School District in Texas (USA), a public school system that fell victim to a successful phishing campaign carried out by cybercriminals. Then, in less than a month, the American cosmetic giant Estée Lauder, leaked onto the Internet nearly 440 million of its internal records as a result of cyber-criminal activities and software security errors. Another incident concerned the Marriott hotel chain, which, as a result of cybercriminal actions, shared the data of about 5.2 million hotel guests. The last situation described here was the need for the University of California to pay a ransom of USD 1.14 million to hackers in June 2020 in order to save its ongoing research on the SARS-CoV-2 (COVID-19) acute respiratory virus.

1   Audit

A theoretical approach

1.1. Audit – definitions, types, objectives, mission

The etymology of the word "audit" dates to distant times and the Latin language, where the terms *auditare* or *audire* meant "to listen" and "to hear" respectively. At the initial stage of the development of the audit, it was indeed the case that it was the auditor who listened carefully to the numbers and bills that were provided to them, i.e., read or dictated, by the accountant. The purpose of such activity was to check the correctness of the numerical records included in the accounts, which reflected settlements of investments or trade between merchants carried out at that time. Thus, audit was a conceptual category that was already known and applied – albeit in a different content and form than is now the case – in all ancient countries, including Mesopotamia, Egypt, Greece, and Rome. Nevertheless, the heyday of auditing came with the expansion of the economic crisis that befell the United States in 1929.[1] Its consequences – both for the United States and for a large part of the world at that time – turned out to be so serious that they initiated a global discussion on the possibility of using audit as a tool to prevent similar economic anomalies in the future.

Until modern times, the concept of audit has received many definitional approaches, which is the result both of the great interest the authors take in it and of the different perspectives with which they approach research on this complex and difficult matter. One of the most general definitions of an audit, provided by Petrascu (2010), describes it as a synthetic process of independent acquisition and evaluation of information, the purpose of which is to assess the degree of its compliance with pre-established criteria and then communicate the results of this work to the interested parties of the process. The concept of auditing is similarly defined by the international Association of Chartered Certified Accountants (ACCA).[2] This group also identifies audit with the process of collecting and analyzing data, in a prede-fined context, whose task is to identify facts (evidence) related to a specific

DOI: 10.4324/9781003380184-2

dispute and provide preventive advice in a specific area. The disputes mentioned in this definition may take on a different nature and relate to irregularities in legal, financial, or ethical aspects. A more descriptive and narrow character of this concept is presented by Gary and Mason (2008), who argue that audit is an activity related to the investigation or search for evidence, which makes it possible to form an opinion on the veracity and reliability of the financial or other information held by a person or persons not directly related to (independent of) a given case. Thanks to this approach, the information obtained during auditing tasks is characterized by greater credibility and usefulness. In the context of the presented definitions of auditing, which by no means exhaust the richness present in subject literature, one can distinguish some general features, which concern the fact that:

- audit is a process[3] aimed at collecting, processing (analyzing), and evaluating information, in order to obtain reasonable assurance as to its compliance and reliability with specific criteria,
- audit, although most often identified within financial and accounting issues, may also concern legal, organizational, moral, or ethical matters,
- audit is a deliberate action to determine the facts, including those resulting from the accounting records, reports, procedures, or strategies of a given organization,
- audit is an independent activity,
- audit is a preventive activity,
- audit is an advisory activity aimed at formulating recommendations and recommendations that should be implemented in the reports prepared by the auditor.

In theoretical and practical terms, the audit may take various forms and types, which are determined by the scope of the adopted criterion. Pająk (2008), taking as criteria the subject of the audit, its level, scope, scope, and stage of research in this area, provides a typology, presented in Table 1.1.

The types of audits presented in Table 1.1, which can be conventionally treated as the basic and most used ones, do not exhaust the long list that has been developed over many years in this field. In practice, it was created by the scientific community researching this area as well as by organizations or individuals who carried out several audit tasks in various areas of life. As an example, it is worth mentioning other types of audits that are referred to by Costello (2003), such as compliance audit, effectiveness and performance audit, legal audit, or contract audit or by Jenkins (1992), who writes about the audit of industrial premises, site contamination audit, or audit of the impact of pollution on the environment. In recent years, popularity has increased for the latter types of audits, which can be described as

Table 1.1 Typology of audits

Criterion	Type
Audit entity	External audit
	Internal audit
Audit subject	Research and development audit
	Financial audit
	Logistic audit
	Marketing audit
	Personnel audit
	Production audit
Audit level	Strategic audit
	Operational audit
Audit scope	Organizational structure audit
	Process audit
	Organizational culture audit
	Audit of results
Audit coverage	Audit of the company
	Audit of the organization's basic subsystems
	Audit of the organizational unit
	Audit of the organizational unit
	Audit of the organizational post/position
Scope of research	Preliminary audit
	Basic audit

Source: Pająk, 2008, p. 71.

environmental. This is mainly due to the global promotion of environmental priorities, which most companies have decided to use as an excellent source of competitive advantage[4] on the market. Bearing in mind the above, we can see that the number of types of audits can be unlimited, because each area of the economy or area of life can be subject to audit activity, which in turn will lead to the creation of new names for the types of audits performed. Nevertheless, practitioners (auditors) who provide audit services on a daily basis divide audit into three main categories:

- financial audit – in which accounting auditors provide opinions on financial statements in terms of their compliance with accounting rules and standards,
- compliance audit – in which auditors verify whether the subject and scope of the audit is consistent with applicable laws, adopted procedures, and policies,
- operational audit – in which the subject, coverage, and scope of the audit can be discretionary or arbitrary.

At this point it should be clearly emphasized that audit, as an advisory and verification activity, is not legally obligatory for all types of organizations or institutions. The catalogue of organizations, or more precisely the areas that are subject to auditing, is – in most countries – regulated by law at the level of national legislation and related regulations. This means that in the case of, for example, Polish legislation,[5] the annual financial statements of entities such as banks or joint-stock companies are subject to mandatory audit (i.e., financial audit), while other organizations are either exempt from this obligation or must meet certain conditions in employment, assets, or net income in order to be subject to it. In other words, it can be concluded that no type of audit is obligatory for any organization, unless the obligation to carry it out results from the provisions of a national law.

Audit, as a causative action aimed at influencing the wider network of socio-economic relations, has certain goals to achieve. In the majority of subject publications those goals are clearly and precisely defined. Thanks to this, stakeholders know what they can expect from conducting audit activities in each area, both in the short and long term. Table 1.2 presents core audit objectives in the context of the role assigned to it in the financial and operational sphere of the economy. At the same time, it should be remembered that these goals are subject to constant evolution (change), due to the development of business models and techniques.

Table 1.2 Core audit objectives

Objectives	Tasks
Main objective	Determination of the reliability of the presented financial and operational information, with the facts.
	Ensuring that the organization's accounts and transactions reflect its true and fair image.
	Formulation of an independent opinion on the reliability and honesty of information obtained during audit tasks.
Auxiliary objectives	Detection and prevention of fraud concerning manipulation and embezzlement of funds, falsification of financial data and so-called sensitive data, improper application and interpretation of applicable legal regulations.
	Detection and elimination of financial and operational errors.
	Identification of processes requiring improvement (improvement of efficiency).
	Assessment of compliance of the functioning of the organization and the tasks performed by it with all applicable provisions of national and/or international law.
	Determination of the effectiveness of the procedures and policies present in the organization.
	Analysis and evaluation of the scope of professional responsibility and duties specified in a given position.

Source: Authors' own study.

In addition to the objectives listed in Table 1.2, audit also has a specific mission to fulfill, which, depending on its type, may take different forms.[6] In practice, the audit mission differs from its objectives; it is not intended to achieve specific results in a given organization but to build a sense of community in thinking about audit as a tool in the area of management and finance that helps organizations and individuals to be reliable and honest partners in creating business networks valuable to the economy. And, just as ACCA's mission is to shape future leaders of the business world and to share specialist and expert knowledge, as well as to promote high professional standards, the mission of any audit should be to make the economic world better and more valuable, which can be realized through:

- supporting the management functions of organizations and institutions through continuous and multi-level evaluation,
- identification and monitoring of irregularities and emerging risks (threats) resulting from the conducted activity, and then their consistent reduction or elimination,
- initiating changes and presenting proposals for improvement, as a mechanism for self-improvement,
- the protection of employees, assets, and information, which are valuable resources for any organization.

The issues presented in this section of the chapter concerning the definition, types, objectives, and mission that audit must fulfill introduce further considerations about the logistics audit and the functions it has to fulfill in the context of a system as complex as the economy. Thanks to the conceptual instruments presented in this section, the reader can move on to further issues related to the audit, which will be characterized by an increasing degree of detail and span. The next section discusses the differences and similarities between external and internal audit, taking into account the subjective criterion of the audit (see Table 1.1).

1.2. External audit *vs.* internal audit – similarities and differences

The subjective criterion adopted in literature on the topic, in the context of the types of audits (see Table 1.1), divides audit into external and internal. It is the most well-known and cardinal division that we deal with when it comes to audit. At the outset, to understand the essence of this division, including its similarities and differences, it is necessary to define both types. One of the definitions of external audit proposed by Satka (2017) states that it is an audit that is carried out by third parties to, for example, verify the correctness of presented financial statements. At the same time – as the author quickly adds – external audit is not limited by anything, so its scope of activity may exceed the generally accepted framework. In other words, it can refer to other aspects of the organization's functioning, not necessarily related to accounting or finance. A slightly different definition is proposed by Nasta and Ladar (2015), in which they not only describe what an external audit is and what is aimed at but also what its primary duty is. According to these authors, the external audit is carried out with the help of independent and external entities and is aimed at conducting a financial analysis along with an assessment of its risk to the organization's activities. In addition, it is primarily addressed to the organization's stakeholders, to obtain reliable information on the financial situation of the company. On the other hand, the main obligation of an external audit is to conduct an annual audit of financial statements, with the purpose of issuing an opinion on the correctness or irregularity of the company's financial situation. One of the most well-known and most cited definitions of external audit is the one proposed by the Chartered Institute of Management Accountants (CIMA).[7] Representatives of this organization – in a narrow sense – define external audit as periodic audits of documentation and accounting operations of entities by a person, who is an auditor,[8] in order to maintain correctness, reliability, honesty, applicable accounting standards, and legal requirements in the image of financial statements of entities. In opposition to the definition proposed by CIMA, the one by Larcker,[9] who – in broad terms – considers external audit to be nothing more than an assessment of the importance and credibility of publicly reported financial information. At the same time – as Larcker clearly emphasizes – the management of the organization is responsible for preparing financial reports, and shareholders[10] expect only impartial information about the company, which will come from independent people. The above definitions of external audit – despite their interpretative diversity – have many common features. They mainly concern the fact that external audit is most often identified with activities that are not only independent and reliable but are, above all, related to the periodic analysis of financial statements and accounts of entities. In practice, this means that external audit is almost always identified with the financial sphere – and, more specifically, accounting – of a given organization, and less often with its operational or managerial sphere. What's more, it is an action, by a given organization (enterprise managers), aimed at fulfilling the provisions of the accounting law in force in this domain as well as the competences to reliably inform shareholders about the financial situation of the company. What is often included in the definition of an external audit is the important role to be played by the person of the auditor, i.e., an independent expert whose task is to obtain reliable information on the financial situation of the enterprise and issue an appropriate report in this respect.

Different than external auditing is the concept of an internal audit, which – especially over the last two decades[11] – has taken on both academic and functional significance. According to the definition of the Institute of Internal Auditors (IIA),[12] internal audit[13] is seen as an independent and objective activity aimed at bringing added value that improves the functioning of a specific organization. Improvement in this area is to take place by increasing the efficiency of processes, identifying and reducing risks or systematic supervision over implemented projects. An extremely concise and precise definition of this conceptual category is proposed by Montgomery (1956), who presents internal audit as an independent evaluation function established in an organization to examine and evaluate its activities. However, as Montgomery observes, internal audit is a form of advisory service provided to a specific organization, which is non-obligatory. Swinkels (2012), examining the theoretical aspects of internal audit in relation to the control systems in force in Dutch listed companies, stated that, in fact, internal audit focuses on activities certifying certain data and information, as well as on consultative work. This would mean that internal audit has – among others – an important proactive (initiating) function in relation to the client's needs, in areas related to control, management, risk, and monitoring, without losing its independence and credibility. Definitions of internal audit by other authors, including Hermanson et al. (2008), draw attention – as was the case with the definition of external audit – to the role played by internal auditors. Thanks to their qualifications in the field of management, risk management, or internal control, they work on achieving the required level of compliance with the law in force in each organization or with adopted procedures and policies. In addition to features associated with independence and objectivity of functioning, the definitions of internal audit presented above are connected by the fact that they are clearly focused on activities in the managerial and operational sphere rather than the financial sphere of the organization. Thus, internal audit is an activity that covers a much wider range of activities than an external audit. However, the number of differences between external and internal audit is much richer and is presented in Table 1.3.

In light of the presented differences between external and internal audits, one should not draw the conclusion that these are types of audits that are in competition with each other; these are areas that, particularly from the point of view of organization, complement each other and form an important aspect of the means to its improvement. Thus, both external and internal audits are important for every organization regardless of its size, scope of activity, or the industry in which it operates. What's more, the

Table 1.3 External audit versus internal audit – comparative approach

External audit	Internal audit
The purpose of an external audit is to verify the correctness of the prepared financial statements	The purpose of internal audit is to bring added value to improve the functioning of the organization
An external audit is an *ex post* audit (follow-up audit)	Internal audit is primarily an *ex ante* audit (prior audit)
An external audit is performed by people from outside the organization	Internal audit can be performed by people from the organization.
An external audit is often "incidental" and is performed once a year	Internal audit is permanent
An external audit focuses on identifying fraud and irregularities in an organization's financial statements	Internal audit focuses on identifying and preventing fraud and irregularities
External audit concerns accounting and bookkeeping activities	Internal audit concerns business and management activities
The implementation of an external audit related to the audit of accounting books is most often obligatory and results from the provisions of applicable law	The implementation of internal audit is voluntary and discretionary
External audit examines the financial aspects of business activity	Internal audit examines all aspects of business activity
External audit scope is limited	The scope of internal audit is unlimited
External audit is carried out on the basis of applicable national legislation (especially the accounting act)	Internal audit is carried out on the basis of applicable procedures and policies adopted in the organization
External audit has a limited impact on the improvement of the organization	Internal audit is the basic tool for improving an organization in all its aspects
External audit has an advisory and verification function	Internal audit has an advisory, verification, control, and proactive function
External audit focuses mainly on finance and accounting departments	Internal audit focuses on all departments in the organization, procedures, and their functions
The value provided to the organization by an external audit is the accuracy, correctness, and reliability of the prepared financial statements and the accounting books kept	The value provided to the organization by internal audit is the operational efficiency of the organization
External audit concerns the operational level in the organization	Internal audit can concern the strategic, operational, and tactical level of the organization
The auditor is elected by the board of directors (management) of the company	The auditor is elected by the management of the company or by the shareholders

(*Continued*)

Table 1.3 (Continued)

External audit	Internal audit
The external auditor does not know the organization well and gets acquainted with it during the implementation of audit tasks	The internal auditor knows the organization well – they are its employee
The external auditor has extensive experience in the implementation of audit tasks	The internal auditor may not have sufficient knowledge and experience in the performance of audit tasks
The main standards for external auditors in the course of their work are International Accounting Standards (IAS) and International Financial Reporting Standards (IFRS)	The main standards for internal auditors in the course of their work are International Standards for Professional Practice of Internal Audit, institute of Internal Auditors (IIA standards)
Auditor – statutory auditor	Auditor – internal auditor
External audit qualifications – certificates such as ACCA, CFA*	Internal audit qualifications – certificates such as CIA**, CISA***
Objectivism	The risk of lack of objectivity
High implementation costs	Low implementation costs

Source: Authors' own elaboration based on secondary research.
*Chartered Financial Analyst (CFA), ** Certified Internal Auditor (CIA), *** Certified Information Systems Auditor (CISA).

interpenetration of similarities in the context of these two types of audits can be observed on many levels, related to:

- autonomy of action – both external and internal audits are characterized by freedom of action and a high degree of independence. In practice, it boils down to the fact that the work carried out as part of each audit is free from prejudice, impartial and objective, avoiding conflicts of interest, and conducted with due diligence within the framework of applicable standards,
- objectives – the basic goal of the external and the internal audit is primarily to identify errors and detect fraud in the organization's activities,
- reporting - the results of both types of audits are formally prepared reports on their implementation in the form of post-audit reports
- planning – all stages related to the implementation of both external and internal audit are carried out in the same, clearly defined and uniform, way. Thus, everything starts with the preparation of audit plans and ends with the publication of reports after those plans have been carried out,
- testing – both financial auditors and internal auditors verify the correctness of, for example, transactions or processes using a tool such as validation (testing),

- risk – is the basic conceptual category that constantly accompanies the implementation of objectives and tasks resulting from conducting external and internal audits,
- work standards – both types of audit must be carried out at a high substantive and organizational level so that they guarantee the reliability and correctness of the results achieved. In this context, international standards of external and internal audit practice, which have been issued by professional organizations and which, in many areas, e.g., related to professional ethics, are convergent with each other.

The similarities presented above may therefore constitute a certain proof regarding the existence of complementarity in the relationship between external and internal audit. Its practical application – especially in the context of improving the effectiveness and quality of operation – could primarily benefit the entire organization because, as Pop et al. (2008) rightly point out:

- internal audit is complementary to external audit, because in organizations where internal audit has already been implemented, external audit is more determined to appreciate, in a different manner, the correct and reliable view of financial results and reports,
- external audit is complementary to an internal audit, since an external audit carried out by persons from outside the organization guarantees the existence of a higher level of control in the organization.

In view of the above, it should also be borne in mind that the existing relational links between external and internal audits are constantly changing and continue to do so. The sources of such links are global megatrends[14] (civilization trends) with high impact, related to Industry 4.0, digitalization, digitization, development of 5G networks, globalization, or electromobility. Therefore, external and internal audits are also undergoing transformation, creating the next generations of audit, which will be discussed in more detail later in the book.

1.3. Evolution of internal audit against the background of audit generation

Evolution is an ambiguous concept. According to Czachorowski (2010), it can mean: any change, a gradual change – which is not abrupt, a change of a fixed direction – which should be associated with finalism,[15] or a change which should be identified with progress, i.e., the transition from simple to more complex forms, marked by superiority and better characteristics.

Speaking about the evolution of internal audit, or more broadly the generation of internal audit (see Figure 1.2), it should be identified primarily with a change of a gradual, not revolutionary nature,[16] which constantly transforms the audit process toward what is newer, more adequate, but also more complex. However, importantly, this change should not be associated with finality (even indirectly), because we would have to adopt the view that the development of audit tends toward some final – undefined – goal or a previously set limit. Meanwhile, auditing is a matter whose development is not subject to any restrictions, and this means that anticipating any goal to which it is ultimately intended is a task that is not merely difficult but is, in practice, impossible. Undoubtedly, time is also required for something to change or transform. Without it, it is difficult for us to judge whether something has changed or not. The passage of time is, for us, a point of reference, thanks to which we can compare things with each other or objectively refer to something. In the case of the evolution that internal audit has experienced over many years (see Figure 1.1), we can say that its content, form, scope of activity, functions, and the role it performs in the area of finance and

1950	Internal audit is primarily focused on accounting
1960	Internal audit focuses on both accounting and operations
1970	A change in the perception of the internal audit area as an activity directed also at the area of operations
1980	Change of the definition of internal audit from "service for management" to "service for the organization". Raising internal audit to the high rank of the audit function
1990	Introducing the concepts of "auditor independence" and "compliance with professional ethics standards". Changing the role of audit towards compliance determination and advisory function
2000	Internal audit increases its interest in the area of corporate governance
2010	More attention paid to the compliance of regulations - especially in the area of data protection and consumer rights - with the provisions of the law introduced after the financial crisis of 2008.
2020	Adding more principles to the international framework for the professional practice of internal audit

Figure 1.1 Evolution of the role of internal audit – 1950–2020 (in decades) Source: Authors' own study based on RSM International Association, 2019, p. 9, and Buła, 2015a, p. 126.

management of each organization are, over the passage of time, subject to change.

The source of their transformation was primarily the business environment, whose elements in the form of dynamics of economic growth, level of competitiveness, technological challenges, information security, efficiency improvement, aspirations of employees and management, complexity of business activity, legal regulations and procedures, as well as levels and types of risk, have always strongly determined the environment in which internal audit is created and shaped. As a consequence, nowadays it has come to the point that internal audit – especially its role and functions – has been significantly expanded, and at almost all levels of the organization. Today, in times of great political and economic turbulence,[17] it plays a strategic role, providing a continuous overview of business processes and risk areas. Thanks to this, it provides timely valuable information to all stakeholders operating in the organization's environment about the functioning of operational and control mechanisms in it.

The result of the evolution of audit (including internal and external) has been the parallel creation at the global level of its subsequent generations (see Figure 1.2). In practice, these were and still are models of functioning and conducting audit tasks characteristic of a given period or epoch, which, taking into account political, economic, and technological conditions, ultimately determined the form of audit. In the subject literature, the following generations of audit are distinguished (Dai & Vasarhelyi, 2016):

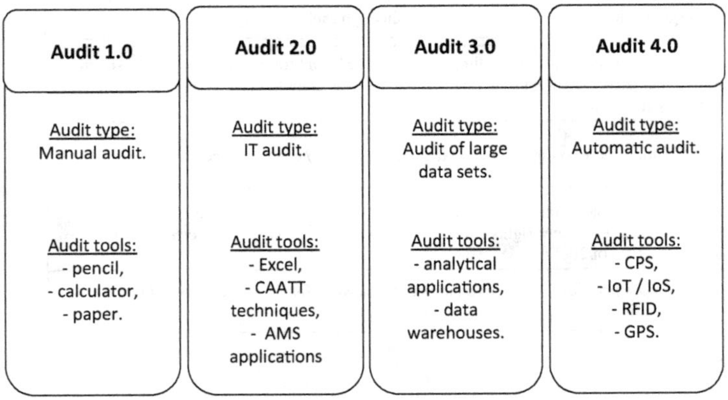

Audit 1.0	Audit 2.0	Audit 3.0	Audit 4.0
Audit type: Manual audit.	Audit type: IT audit.	Audit type: Audit of large data sets.	Audit type: Automatic audit.
Audit tools: - pencil, - calculator, - paper.	Audit tools: - Excel, - CAATT techniques, - AMS applications	Audit tools: - analytical applications, - data warehouses.	Audit tools: - CPS, - IoT / IoS, - RFID, - GPS.

Figure 1.2 Generations of audit – from the past to the present Source: Authors' own study based on Dai and Vasarhelyi, 2016, p. 2.

- Audit 1.0 – the first generation of audit was born with the creation of the IIA in 1941.[18] All audit tasks at that time were performed in a traditional way, i.e., manually. The tools used by the auditors in their work were characterized by extraordinary simplicity and were a pencil, a sheet of paper, a pen, and a calculator (previously an abacus). Audit 1.0 focused its attention more on *ex post* activities than *ex ante,*
- Audit 2.0 – the second generation of audit came with the development of the first era of computerization, which occurred in the 1980s and 1990s, when the first desktop computers became available to ordinary users. Audit 2.0 is referred to as an *IT audit* because IT tools were used for the first time in the form of various types of applications and IT systems, such as Excel, CAATT, or AMS. The CAATT (Computer Assisted Audit Tools and Techniques) system was one of the first IT tools supporting the work of auditors. The same applies to AMS (Audit Management Software), which was a tool used to manage audit tasks. Nowadays, there are more extensive and innovative solutions in the area of these two applications,[19]
- Audit 3.0 – the third generation of audit falls on the first years of the 21st century. Its creation was related to the geometrically growing amount of data and information across the world, which needed to be organized, also in terms of newly emerging risk areas. Hence the idea of the big-data audit, which focused its attention on the review and analysis of selected systems collecting important – from the point of view of the functioning of the organization – data. The new environment in which audit functioned at the beginning of the 21st century also required the use of new tools in the approach to audit tasks, whether in the form of data warehouses or so-called analytical applications (business intelligence systems).
- Audit 4.0 – the fourth generation of audit came at the end of the first decade of the 21st century and should be directly identified with the development of the Fourth Industrial Revolution (Industry 4.0) – a phenomenon that increases the turbulence of the organization's business environment as a result of the permanent development of modern technologies and innovations. The final shape of Audit 4.0 will depend, in a significant way, on the development and innovative technologies promoted by Industry 4.0[20] in the form of cyber-physical systems (CPS), the Internet of Things (IoT), the Internet of Services (IoS), identification of objects using radio waves (Radio-Frequency Identification, RFID), or satellite navigation system (Global Positioning System, GPS). In practice, Audit 4.0 will be a process consisting in the objective collection of information from the Internet, cyber-physical systems, and intelligent (autonomous)

machines and devices that, after analysis and visualization, will identify patterns and deviations from the desired state. Importantly, Audit 4.0 will continue to draw on the experience of Audit 3.0, especially in data analysis and obtaining information necessary for the entire audit task. In light of growing global digitization and digitization of economic life, the skills of auditors will also have to undergo a radical change, who from now on will carry out audit tasks – related to the verification of processes, procedures and transactions – in the environment of intelligent (autonomous) machines, devices, or entire factories.

The audit generations presented above are, in fact, a reflection of the changes that organizations have undergone over the past several decades. Their source was technological progress, which determined the way enterprises function and are managed. The situation is similar today, when innovation and digital transformation[21] are penetrating faster and deeper into various spheres of economic life and all industries, thus posing new challenges to organizations. Consequently, there are changes in the methods of production, in supply chain management, in the organizational structures of enterprises, in the work environment, in interpersonal communication, in data management, or in business models. Importantly, the way of perceiving and managing risk, which is an inseparable element of running any business, is also changing. These changes and challenges require an appropriate audit response, since such a response also needs to be transformed to meet the tasks for which it was formed. What is more, it must be prepared to reliably assess the processes, procedures, or transactions that will be carried out in the new, digital reality. However, this situation may give rise to the risk of audit inaction. Therefore, it must also actively respond to changes taking place in the organization, so that it can continue to play a preventive role in relation to the new risks to which it will be exposed. The transformational changes taking place at various levels of the organization, as well as in its various cells or departments, will also require greater commitment both on the part of the entire management and of the employees. In the case of people responsible for managing the organization, it is not only about using new technologies in audit work, but also about developing a new model that will consider and use the possibilities offered by digital technology, e.g., in the area of analysis of large data sets. In other words, it is about defining a new generation audit that will take into account aspects related to innovation (e.g., the use of artificial intelligence in audit),[22] efficiency, effectiveness of using large data resources, and improvement of risk management.

1.4. Internal audit and controlling – a comparative analysis

Based on management and finance sciences, the issue regarding the occurrence of differences and similarities in relation to internal audit and controlling[23] has been subject to many interpretations and definitions. In practice – paradoxically – this led to a blurring of the essence of both issues, which meant that internal audit and controlling were often treated as synonyms. In addition, it is also not difficult to identify in subject literature the cases in which both these conceptual categories are used interchangeably. Meanwhile, internal audit is not controlling, just as controlling is not internal audit, even though both terms have certain features that are common to each. This section will attempt, for the sake of terminological order, to sort out the essence, differences, and similarities between internal audit and controlling. However, more emphasis will be placed on the issue of controlling, as the concept of internal audit has already been described in more detail in Sections 1.2 and 1.3. However, it should start with the fact that in recent years controlling has become an important tool for influencing the processes taking place in the organization and one of the main instruments shaping the correct "attitudes" in its daily functioning. This is mainly due to the development of the organizational environment, as well as the increase in the popularity of scientific concepts aimed at the continuous improvement and efficient functioning of the institution. In practice, the increased importance of controlling has been reflected in the richness of terms and concepts describing what controlling is, how it should be interpreted in a broad or narrow sense, or what forms it can take based on governing and managing an organization. Controlling is most often defined in management literature as a process thanks to which the management strives to acquire and use the limited resources of the organization as effectively as possible in order to implement the adopted strategy of action. In addition, the frequently cited definitions of controlling also indicate that it is one of the four basic management functions, along with planning, organizing, and motivating. From this perspective, it can be concluded – and rightly so – that controlling, and, in fact, its result, is also the basic determinant of success in the functioning of any organization. Finally, controlling should – as should several of the management functions – be carried out at all levels of the organization in a permanent or periodic manner, so that the management staff can be sure that the tasks performed within the adopted strategy ultimately serve its implementation. The most common definitions of controlling in the literature are presented in Table 1.4.

A careful reading of scientific studies in the field of management in general, and controlling and internal audit in particular, allows us to see that the term "controlling"[24] can be used both in a narrow and a broad sense.

Table 1.4 Definitions of controlling – a literature review

Definitions of controlling	Author/Source
Controlling is one of the management functions performed by managers at all levels of the organization. They are responsible for the tasks assigned to be performed, and at the same time they exercise regular control over subordinates so that the set goals can be achieved	Cambalikova and Misun, 2017
The essence of controlling is not to "assess" whether the planned goals have been achieved but to monitor the progress in achieving the goals	Sljivic et al., 2015
Controlling at the micro- and macroeconomic levels is an essential management function	Ionescu, 2010
Controlling means a comparison between the planned and actual activity, together with the identification of possible corrective actions	Herath, 2007
Controlling is the process of directing a set of variables in order to achieve the assumed result. It's a broad term applicable to people, things, situations, and organizations. In organizations, controlling includes various planning and supervision processes	Anthony et al., 1989
Controlling, as a word referring to the function of management, is about influencing human behavior, because it is people who make something happen in the organization. In other words, controlling is when managers take steps to ensure that people are doing the best for the organization	Merchant, 1985
Controlling processes help to reduce idiosyncratic behavior and maintain its compliance with the rational plan of the organization	Tannenbaum, 1962

Source: Authors' own study.

In a narrow sense, Krzyżanowski (1994) defines controlling as a set of specific activities that consist of examining actual states with tasks, finding deviations, and formulating recommendations, without including them in the scope of corrective and regulatory procedures that belong to the preceding functions. Such an approach to controlling, as Bielińska-Dusza (2011) rightly points out, is strictly reporting and advisory. This means that this type of controlling focuses primarily on establishing the factual situation, which takes place by measuring a given phenomenon in relation to designated paradigms or norms, and then focuses on formulating recommendations to correct the aberrations created in the organization. As part of the narrow approach to controlling,[25] Lisiński (2011) distinguishes the following forms: inventory (so-called physical inventory), overview (preliminary inspection), visitation (direct controlling), safeguarding (direct controlling of the "object"), surveillance (discreet controlling of the "object"), checking (verification), inspection (state control, departmental control, etc.), audit (supplementing current controlling), internal audit, insight (view of the phenomenon), review (check), monitoring (observation and measurement of the phenomenon), internal controlling (process), internal control system (activities, tasks). In broad terms, however, controlling is defined as an activity whose purpose is only to check whether the execution agrees with the plan, i.e., the previously adopted pattern (Adamiecki, 1985). With regard to the organization and its management, it boils down to the systematic supervision of its main representatives over the implementation of the proper course of previously planned activities within the defined strategy.

The broad approach to control differs from its narrow approach in that the authorities supervising or managing a given institution can directly influence its nature and scope, but at the same time they bear greater responsibility for their actions and/or omissions. As part of this approach to control, the following forms are distinguished (Lisiński, 2011): supervision (including the so-called corporate supervision), controlling,[26] self-assessment, and compliance.[27]

Having a basic understanding of the essence of internal audit (see Section 1.2) and controlling, we can see that although they are close and related concepts, they are characterized by a certain distinctiveness. Nevertheless, on the basis of both theory and practice, it is not uncommon to encounter the thesis that audit and control are two completely different activities. As proof of its support, an image is presented (see Figure 1.3) of the controller and the auditor, standing back-to-back, where one looks to the past and the other to the future. Looking into the past is the person of the controller, and into the future, the auditor. Meanwhile – apart from the suggestions contained in the figure – one cannot evaluate audit and controlling in terms

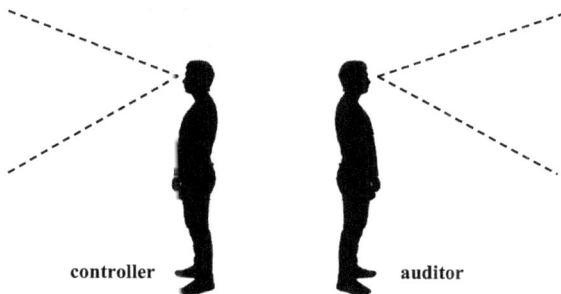

Figure 1.3 Audit *vs.* controlling – graphic approach Source: Authors' own study.

of black-and-white thinking. These are two conceptual terms which, despite their distinctiveness, have common features and areas that are characteristic of them and which are subject to mutual interpenetration. As an example, it is worth mentioning that both internal audit and controlling are instruments used by management to control risk in the organization or to protect the company's assets against the undesirable actions of its employees or third parties.

In the context of the above, it should be noted that internal audit and controlling are related but still separate terms. There are more differences between them than similarities (see Table 1.5). As an exemplification, it should be emphasized that the starting points for activities in internal audit are the potential risks that are an inherent feature of the organization's functioning in any environment (especially turbulent), while controlling activities are triggered as a result of the existence of irregularities or fraud. Besides, internal audit is a process-oriented activity, not a people-oriented one. Thus, unlike inspections, it seeks to detect inconsistencies inherent in the processes or procedures of the organization and does not focus on detecting and punishing employees guilty of negligence. Consequently, the psychological reaction of employees to the audit and control should also be different – at least in theory. While the auditee will rather hide inconvenient work-related facts, the person who is the subject of audit activities will be inclined to cooperate with the auditor, which should result in providing them with comprehensive information about the functioning of the organization. In addition, audit tasks – implemented constantly and systematically – are carried out through interviews with employees and research and analysis of both documents and systems, while controlling activities – undertaken at random – are carried out using instruments in the form of visitation, revision, inspection, or monitoring. A detailed account of the differences between internal audit and controlling is provided in Table 1.5.

At the end of this section, it is worth mentioning that both internal audit and controlling are those instruments supporting the management of the organization, which should be used in a thoughtful manner that is adequate to the situation. In particular, this applies to controlling, the excess of which may have a negative impact on the efficiency of company operations, which in an extreme case may even lead to a slowdown in its development and even, ultimately, collapse. Therefore, the instruments supporting organization management must be permanently adapted to the specifics and individual requirements of each organization. At the same time, it should be borne in mind that an organization may exist without an audit, but without controlling, it may not.

Table 1.5 Internal audit and controlling – differences

Internal audit	Controlling
The starting point for activities in the area of internal audit are potential and critical risks resulting from the functioning of a given organization	The starting point for controlling activities in the organization are suspicions related to the existence of irregularities
Independent activity, performed by choice	Activity limited by the scope of the permit, performed on commission
It can be *ex ante* or *ex post*	It can only be *ex post*
It provides the management of a given organization with objective information on how it functions in terms of legality, economics, expediency, reliability, transparency, and openness	Provides the management of a given organization with information on the established facts using control criteria
Verification activity	Checking activity
Focused on improvement	Aimed at searching for irregularities
Strives to confirm compliance	It seeks to confirm non-compliance
Oriented to processes, procedures, etc.	People-oriented (personal responsibility)
No sanctions	Sanctions (penalties)
Providing an advisory function	Preventive function
Supports management	It protects the organization against losses
Supports risk management	Reduces and eliminates risk
Carried out constantly and systematically	Carried out at random
Implemented through conversations with employees, document research, analysis of systems and processes	Carried out through visits, revisions, inspections, monitoring
Planned	Unplanned (element of surprise)
An organization can exist without an audit	An organization cannot exist without control
It is carried out by an internal auditor	It is carried out by a controller
The internal auditor often reports directly to the head of the unit, who ensures that the auditor has both organizational and procedural separation in the performance of their audit tasks	The inspection is carried out by an employee of the control unit or, on the basis of a personal authorization, by an employee delegated to this task by the management of the unit
Internal audit practices performed on the basis of international standards	Performed on the basis of internal procedures
Low costs of realization	It does not generate higher costs
Audit report	Report of the inspection carried out

Source: Authors' own study based on secondary research and Buła, 2015a, pp. 141–2.

1.5. Internal auditor – role, tasks, standards, work

The IIA agrees that the main goal of internal audit, as an independent and objective activity, is to increase the value, and improve the functioning, of the organization. In other words, it is simply about improving a thing and/ or processes. This task is carried out primarily through:

- verifying specific items (existing data) and comparing them with established requirements,
- identifying and learning about exceptions,
- review of non-standard things and phenomena,
- reconstruction or correction of identified errors,
- proposing improvements to eliminate exceptions (deviations) in the future,
- assistance in streamlining and stabilizing processes.

The effectiveness and efficiency of the above-mentioned activities that fall within the scope of audit work will depend on the specialist who will carry them out. It is the internal auditor, who is referred to here, that will be responsible for the quality and operability of the audit. To achieve it, an internal auditor must have the right range of skills, knowledge, and knowledge of selected scientific disciplines (e.g., law, management, finance, economics, IT) and be ready to constantly improve their own qualifications, which are somehow connected with the exercise of this profession. In practice, internal auditors are highly trusted researchers, analysts, or advisors who focus on identifying and solving problems that trouble organizations in their daily work. Importantly, they bring to these organizations important values related to matter-of-factness, skills, knowledge, and experience, which constitute a permanent foundation for all internal activities of any company or institution. Nowadays, people who professionally and on a daily basis deal with internal audit, must have, in addition to hard competences (specialist knowledge, knowledge of computer programs and systems, etc.) – as already mentioned – soft competences, i.e., those closely related to the human psyche. This means that the internal auditor must also be able to cope with stress, effectively manage his person, give the ability to self-motivation, and be able to show assertiveness and creativity. In addition, the auditor should have extensive communication skills, such as motivating others to work, delegating tasks, the ability to build and work in a team, or self-presentation skills, so that the auditor can effectively use them in relation with other people, especially during the implementation of audit activities. Soft skills, which allow their owner to behave effectively in certain situations, are nowadays – and not only in relation to the internal auditor profession – of great importance in recruitment processes.[28] Although skills, competences, standards (including standards of professional ethics), and the role played by internal auditors in organizations have already been described in detail and exhaustively in many scientific publications and trade journals, it is still not uncommon for internal auditors to be confused particularly with external auditors but also with accountants and chartered accountants. Meanwhile, the areas of professional interest of both an internal auditor, an external auditor, or an accountant differ – and significantly – from each other, as well as the skills that are needed to perform these professions. The differences between the professions of internal and external auditor are more clearly highlighted in Table 1.6.

In order to supplement the information contained in Table 1.6, it is necessary to recall here 11 basic tasks that have been specified by the IIA and which are carried out by internal auditors in their daily work. They concern (The Institute of Internal Auditors, 2016):

Table 1.6 Internal auditor *vs.* external auditor – scope of activities and competences

Internal auditor	External auditor
Usually employed by the organization in which they work (unless this function is outsourced or as part of periodic cooperation), but the work performed is independent of the area audited	Hired by the organization from the outside, to perform a specific service for it
Wide range of activities:	**Detailed scope of action:**
• risk management • corporate governance • operational and strategic objectives of the organization • operational efficiency and effectiveness • compliance • accuracy of financial statements • process management • other	• correctness of financial statements
Experience and skills:	**Detailed experience and skills:**
• communication skills • interpersonal skills • IT skills • analytical skills (exploration of data) • industry and specialist knowledge• knowledge in the field of accounting	• in bookkeeping and accounting • in auditing accounting books
Ex post and *ex ante* approach	**Mainly *ex post* approach**

Source: Based on The Institute of Internal Auditors, 2016, p. 4, and Buła, 2015a, p. 136.

1) consulting on and verification of projects – the knowledge of internal auditors regarding the mechanisms of the functioning of controlling systems and a holistic view of the organization make them ideal candidates to be project consultants. Thanks to the ability to assess risk, they can take on the role of an advisor who will help solve existing problems. Nevertheless, it is the management that must ultimately take responsibility for the implementation of projects in their areas,

2) risk assessment – due to the fact that the risk is nearly ubiquitous (natural disasters, terrorist and cyberattacks, loss of key suppliers, loss of reputation, fraud, financial embezzlement, lawsuits, violation of legal, moral, and ethical principles), the task of the internal auditor is to identify and assess risk from the point of view of its impact on the functioning of the organization. The auditor should effectively control the risk by transferring knowledge about it to the management of the organization and developing recommendations aimed at its effective management,

3) assessment of controlling (system) – internal auditors assess the efficiency and effectiveness of the functioning of control mechanisms in the organization and issue recommendations to the management as to the correctness of its operation,

4) ensuring accuracy and correctness in the preparation of statements and reports – internal auditors guarantee the reliability and correctness of financial and non-financial statements prepared in the organization. Ensuring accuracy in the reports prepared by the auditors, is made possible by testing the reliability of the information contained in the documents with the facts.

5) process improvement – having knowledge about the organization and its strategic goals, internal auditors analyze the processes and operations taking place in the organization to determine the degree of the efficiency and productivity of the strategic goals,

6) promoting ethical attitudes – professionalism in the internal auditor profession consists in compliance with the principles enshrined in the code of ethics, which guards honesty, reliability, objectivity, and confidentiality in the performance of tasks and audit activities. Thus, detected irregularities should always be subject to appropriate behavior and be reported to the relevant persons, bodies, or institutions,

7) review of processes and procedures – internal auditors examine the correctness of the designed processes and created procedures that are to serve the implementation of both operational and strategic goals of the organization,

8) compliance monitoring – internal auditors assess the degree of compliance of an organization with applicable laws, regulations, contracts, and laws to ensure that senior management meets these requirements. In addition, they monitor the impact of non-compliance on the activities

of the organization and provide information on this subject to the top management,

9) ensuring security – tangible resources (assets), human resources, and intellectual capital (trademarks, patents, etc.) are valuable to any organization and should therefore be subject to special protection and security. Damage caused in this field can, in an extreme case, even lead to the collapse of the organization. Therefore, internal auditors assess the organization's internal procedures to properly protect its assets against theft, fire, or activities inconsistent with applicable law. In addition, they reveal deficiencies in the security systems and recommend better protection of goods,

10) investigating cases of embezzlement and fraud – since fraud (including theft, embezzlement, extortion) can happen in any organization and at any level of it, it is important that the management board grants appropriate powers and powers of attorney to the internal auditor to carry out the so-called audits of detecting economic fraud and investigating possible fraud throughout the organization,

11) communicating work results – after conducting audit activities in a specific area, the internal auditor reports his findings and recommendations to the appropriate organizational unit responsible for their ongoing coordination and supervision.

The scale at which internal auditors carry out the tasks, described above, in the organization depends on several factors, including:

- type of organizational structure (the degree of its management span or the number of management levels),
- stage of development (in the organizational life cycle) at which the organization is located (whether it is the stage of birth, maturity, or maybe aging),
- size of the organization (e.g., micro-enterprise, corporation, holding),
- sector or industry (the organization may operate in the so-called sensitive industry, i.e., fuel, aviation, energy, or gambling),
- legal form of the organization (the legal form of the organization determines the regulations to which it is subject),
- country of origin (national, treaty, international regulations).

With this in mind, we can therefore see that internal auditors have work to do that is not only important and demanding but also covers a wide range of activities to be performed. Consequently, this situation determines the need for internal auditors to have the appropriate knowledge and skills, which is a *sine qua non* condition for the exercise of this profession. According to Sawyer et al. (2003) an internal auditor should have the following qualifications:

- first, the internal auditor should have a thorough knowledge of the standards, procedures, and techniques of internal audit that are necessary for them to perform their work properly. Proficiency is understood here as the ability to properly apply knowledge in situations that may arise and deal with them without the need to constantly refer to research, tests or the help of other people,
- second, the internal auditor should be required to have a very good knowledge of accounting principles and standards, given that they are a person who works intensively with financial documentation and reports,
- third, the internal auditor must have knowledge of the basic principles and functions of management to be able to identify and assess the significance of deviations from good business practices and customs. In fact, it boils down to a situation in which the internal auditor is able to recognize significant deviations (inconsistencies) and, having qualifications, can carry out the research necessary to find the correct solution to the problem,
- fourth, the internal auditor is required to know (a fact signaled earlier) the fundamentals of subjects such as accounting, economics, commercial law, tax law, finance, management, quantitative methods, or IT. Thanks to this, the auditor will be able to quickly identify extensive or potential problems and define their further course in the context of his research,
- fifth, the internal auditor should be skilled in effective forms of communication with others. This will allow the maintenance of proper relationships with customers or other business partners. Proficiency in verbal and written communication will ensure that they will be able to clearly, and effectively, articulate their cases, tasks, assessments, conclusions, or recommendations,
- sixth, persons supervising the work of internal auditors should clearly define the criteria – including the level of education and experience – necessary to occupy positions related to internal audit. In addition, each audit-related position should have the scope of responsibilities and work that have been assigned to it in the context of performing audit activities,
- seventh, in order to meet the requirements of a modern internal audit, people related to it should have certain character traits related to understanding, determination, adaptation, or assertiveness.

The internal auditor profession, which in fact consists of the permanent improvement of existing processes and procedures within the organization, is not only burdensome but also demanding, in terms of better ideas, results, and audit experience. As a result, it is recommended that it be performed in team form, with close cooperation between employees of the entire organization.

1.6. Control and analytical questions

Control questions

1. Explain the etymology of the word "audit" and define its essence.
2. Taking into account the criterion of the subject and the subject of the audit, list its types accordingly.
3. Name the three main categories of audit.
4. Discuss the two main and two auxiliary audit objectives.
5. According to the definition proposed by the Institute of Internal Auditors, internal audit is ...?
6. Name the five main differences between internal and external audit.
7. Briefly discuss the essence of the audit generations, from 1.0 to 4.0.
8. Give a definition of the word "controlling."
9. Give a definition of the word "controlling" in narrow and broad terms.
10. Name the five differences between internal audit and control.
11. List five tasks specified by the Institute of Internal Auditors that are carried out by internal auditors in their daily work.
12. Define the scope of activities and competences of the internal and external auditor.
13. Discuss what is the task of an internal auditor related to ensuring the security of the organization.
14. List three factors determining the scale and scope of audit tasks.
15. Discuss the most important qualifications that Sawyer et al. (2003) think an internal auditor should possess.

Analytical questions

1. If we assume that a mission has a clearly defined, long-term goal that an organization strives for, then what is the mission in the case of an audit?
2. The evolution of internal audit is commonly equated with a change of an evolutionary rather than a revolutionary nature. Demonstrate the validity of this statement by discussing the stages and generations of internal audit development from 1950 to the present day.
3. Give examples that would confirm the thesis that "internal audit is not controlling, just as controlling is not, in fact, an internal audit."

4. In your opinion, is the work as an internal auditor burdensome and is it impossible to perform it without appropriate qualifications? What soft and hard skills should a person who does this type of work have?
5. Discuss the trends and new technologies related to the (internal) audit of the future.

Notes

1 The Great Depression is the largest economic collapse in the history of capitalism, which took place in the United States between 1929 and 1933. It was triggered by a sharp decline on 24 October 1929 (Black Thursday) when the prices of all shares on the New York Stock Exchange (NYSE) collapsed, which led to bankruptcies and massive debts chiefly among the American public.
2 ACCA is the largest international organization in the world, associating specialists in the field of finance, accounting, and bookkeeping. For more information, see www.accaglobal.com.
3 It is a set of interrelated activities (activities or tasks), the implementation of which is a condition *sine qua non* to obtaining a predefined result. Each process, with its beginning and end, is in fact aimed at satisfying the needs of customers, both external and external and internal.
4 Competitive advantage is the achievement by the organization of a superior position over its market competition. An enterprise can achieve a competitive advantage in three main areas: quality, price, information.
5 Article 64(1) of the Polish Accounting Act of 29 September 1994.
6 For more on this subject, see: Kuc B. (2002). *Internal Audit, Theory and Practice*. Wydawnictwo Menedżerskie PTM, Warsaw, 2020, pp. 75–80.
7 Founded in 1919, in the United Kingdom (London), it is the leading and the largest organization in the world, associating specialists in the field of management accounting. Currently, it has more than 232,000 members and is present in 177 countries. For more information on CIMA see: www.cimaglobal.com.
8 A person conducting an audit, having qualifications and skills in this area, often regulated by law.
9 Larcker is a professor of accounting and law at Stanford University (California) in the United States. His research focuses on issues related to corporate governance, accounting management, and compensation agreements in organizations.
10 However, it should be made clear that the enterprise's shareholders are always its stakeholders, while the stakeholders are not always its shareholders.
11 Internal audit has become particularly popular as a result of reforms that have been carried out in the United States since the collapses and financial scandals associated with major corporations such as Enron and WorldCom.
12 The IIA is the oldest and largest auditing organization in the world, founded in 1941, in the United States (New York), bringing together internal auditors. Currently, it has nearly 200,000 members around the world. For more information on the IIA, see www.theiia.org.
13 According to Sawyer, internal audit is a holistic and independent assessment of activities carried out by internal auditors that relates to specific operations and tasks in the organization, mainly in relation to authenticity of financial and

operational information, identification and minimization of risks, the efficiency and effectiveness of the use of available resources, or compliance with procedures, policies, and regulations within a given enterprise (both in terms of the internal and external environments of the organization).

14 The precursor of this conceptual category is considered to be American futurologist John Naisbitt, author of the best-selling book *Megatrends: Ten New Directions Transforming Our Lives*, which sold more than 9 million copies in 60 countries around the world.

15 Synthetically, it is the view that everything is moving toward some ultimate goal.

16 From the point of view of audit development, changes considered as revolutionary are those caused by global financial crises, that cause changes in the laws regarding finance, corporate governance, compliance, accounting, accounting, consumer rights protection privacy, ownership, etc.

17 Such as those related to the outbreak, in early February 2020, of the global COVID-19 pandemic.

18 See endnote 12.

19 For more on this topic, see Szadkowski, B. (2014). Audit support software. *Financial monthly BANK*, July–August, Warsaw.

20 The term "Industry 4.0" first appeared in the public space in 2011, thanks to the industrial fair held in Germany (in Hanover). Use of the term (German original *Industrie 4.0*) was related to the concept of German businessmen, politicians, and scientists who advocated strengthening the competitiveness of German industry in the face of increasing competition from China. Nowadays, in the literature on the subject, we also meet with other forms of the term "Industry 4.0," which should be treated as synonyms, namely: Era of Systems Cyber-Physical (Cyber-Physical System Era, CPSs Era), Industry of the Future, Production of the Future, or 4IR (Fourth Industrial Revolution).

21 Digital transformation is a process that involves transforming business models, optimizing processes implemented in a given organization, building a digital work environment, and changing the current vision of the company. The primary goal of digital transformation is to increase efficiency and reduce risk. For more on this topic, see Ziyadin, S., Suieubayeva, S., and Utegenova, A. (2020). *Digital Transformation in Business*, DOI: 10.1007/978-3-030-27015-5_49.

22 For more on this subject, see American Accounting Association. (2016). Research ideas for artificial intelligence in auditing: the formalization of audit and workforce supplementation, *Journal of Emerging Technologies in Accounting*, 13(2): 1–20, DOI: 10.2308/jeta-10511 and Moffitt, K.C., Rozario, A.M., and Vasarhelyi M. A. (2018). Robotic process automation for auditing, *Journal of Emerging Technologies in Accounting*, 15(1): 1–10, DOI: 10.2308/jeta-10589.

23 Control is a word derived from the French language, from the word *contrerole*, meaning checking, verification, or evaluation.

24 When discussing – in the context of internal audit – the term *controlling*, it is impossible not to mention The Committee of Sponsorship Organizations of the Treadway Commission (COSO), a joint initiative of five private organizations, including the American Accounting Association (AAA), American Institute of Certified Public Accountants (AICP), Financial Executives International (FEI), Institute of Management Accountants (IMA), and the Institute of Internal Auditors (IIA). COSO aims to provide informed leadership in organizations by developing frameworks and guidance on internal control, risk management, and

fraud prevention in enterprises. For more information, see https://www.coso .org/.

25 Cichy (2019) believes that controlling in narrow terms is: comparison plus drawing conclusions from this comparison. For more on this topic, see Cichy, L. (2019). *Management Internal Control in a Public Company in Terms of Comparative Law*. Legal Monographs. C.H. Beck Publishing House, Warsaw.

26 Controlling, in management sciences, is often defined as a new management function. Controlling focuses on the coordination of basic processes taking place in the organization in order to implement the designated operational and strategic tasks.

27 Compliance, in management sciences, is often referred to as compliance management. In practice, it is an activity (tasks) consisting in ensuring the operational activities of the organization with the requirements of national and international law, regulations, procedures, standards, as well as ethical principles applicable in a given sector or industry.

28 For more on this subject, see Ernst & Young (2012). Competences and qualifications sought by employers among university graduates entering the labor market. Results of a survey conducted by the Warsaw School of Economics, the American Chamber of Commerce in Poland and Ernst & Young. Warsaw.

2 Logistics audit

A classical approach

2.1. The enterprise logistics system – definitions, types, treatments

It is an important thesis that to carry out logistics audit activities, it is necessary to have good knowledge of the logistics system existing within a given economic system (organization, sector, or industry), because it is this very logistics system – including the elements that make it up – that is the subject of verification and evaluation through audit. This chapter is devoted to basic issues related to the existence, scheme, and functioning of the logistics system. However, considerations on this subject should begin with the definition of the very concept of "system." At this point, it should be emphasized mainly that the term "system" is often abused and freely interpreted, especially in the area of broadly understood logistics. This is due to the fact that this concept is defined too widely, which, most likely, has roots in ignorance of systems theory.[1] However, setting aside such divagations, we can conventionally accept after Mynarski (1979), that a system is a set of elements and relationships (dependencies connecting individual elements into a whole) occurring both between these elements and their properties (features of individual elements).[2] In the context of the subject matter, however, the definition of the system proposed in 2005 by the European Logistics Organization (ELO)[3] is more useful – the system is the place in which processes of movement of goods and/or persons occur, where this action is aimed at profit (as is the case in production and commercial enterprises). In this case we are dealing with the so-called economic system, while where the action is not focused on generating profit, as is the case of public institutions, we are dealing with a system of non-profit institutions.

With a general understanding of what a system is, we can now move on to trying to define what a logistics system is. Malindžák et al. (2015) consider that the logistics system (cf. Figure 2.1) is a system that manages, ensures, and implements the flow of materials, information, and financial

DOI: 10.4324/9781003380184-3

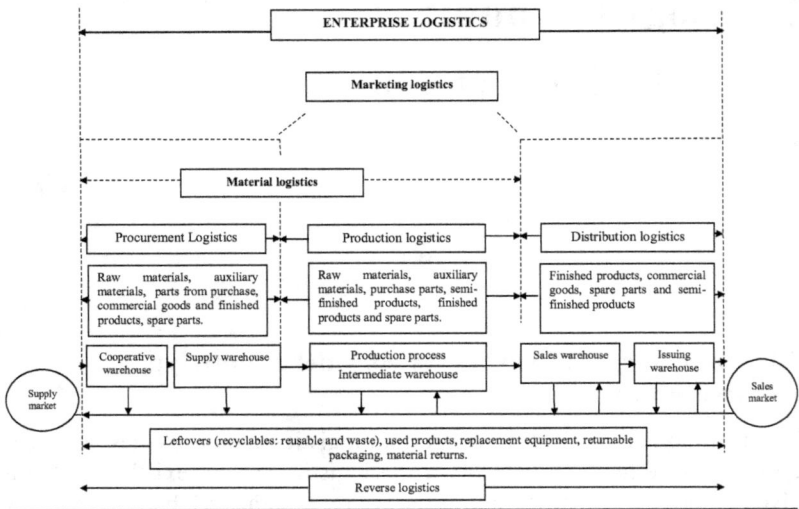

Figure 2.1 The logistics system of the organization in a functional cross-section – graphic approach Source: (Mroczko, 2016, p. 136)

resources. However, they quickly add that, in order to properly define its levels – as a hierarchical system – then, from the point of view of systems theory, it is necessary to first determine the position of the observer (i.e., whether it is a person looking at the organization from within or from the outside). Blaik (2001) presents a similarly broad view of the logistics system presents, considering it to be a set of logistical elements whose connections are formalized and fixed through the processes of transformation taking place. At the same time, he emphasizes that between these elements – with specific features – there occur close and detailed connections (in the organizational sense). A certain complement to the definitions of logistics systems quoted above is the one proposed by Słowiński (2008), who believes that the logistics system is deliberately organized and integrated in the flow of materials and products, and besides, it is an open system because logistics in every aspect is combined with the market and the customer. What all the definitions of a logistics system have in common is that the authors often emphasize the fact that it is not only a connected and integrated system but also consists of many elements, which in practice are reflected mainly in subsystems, including procurement, production, storage, transport, distribution, disposal, planning, steering/guiding, organization, or control. On the other hand, processes take place between the characteristics of individual subsystems that determine the flow of financial resources and information.

When undertaking to characterize a logistics system from the point of view of definitions existing in the literature, one should also know that we can look at a logistics system from both the technical and the functional side (Malindžák et al., 2015). In technical terms, the elements of this system are tools and devices that ensure movement (the flow of people/goods in time and place) including cars, aircraft, ships, railway, conveyors, storage equipment, production lines, robots, transport platforms, cranes, forklifts, transport signaling (e.g., bells).

In the case of material flow, these will be terminals, computers, IT networks, modems, satellites, digital and transmission devices. Speaking about the flow of information, we are dealing with material, information, and financial flows. As far as the functional approach is concerned, in the logistics system it is reflected in the allocation, location, organization, management, and coordination of the flow of materials, products, information, and financial resources. In practice, these are important activities related to the allocation and spatial planning of the organization, including production machinery and equipment, distribution or sales centers, selection of suppliers of products and services, determination of production capacity, preparation of production plans, development of operational and financial plans, design of warehouse space, etc. According to Malindžák et al. (2015), all these activities are closely related and form a chain related to the flows of various objects that are subject to management and which make up the logistic system of functions. In this way, the logistics system (its elements) is finally created,[4] which, according to Kiperska-Moroń and Krzyżaniak (2009), defines:

- the way in which logistics processes take place,
- a set of techniques for carrying out logistics processes,
- a set of means by which logistics processes are carried out.

Like any system, the logistics system is also characterized by specific properties and features, among which we can distinguish primarily those related to:

- a high degree of consistency – in practice this means that a change made within one subsystem automatically entails changes in the other subsystems. This situation is dictated by the fact that there is a high degree of correlation between the various subsystems and the elements that make up it,
- a high level of flexibility – which is reflected in the response of the logistics system to changes taking place in the organizational environment of the enterprise (both internal and external).

At this point, it should also be added that logistics systems are subject to many divisions in the subject literature. One of the most popular is related to the spatial location of logistics systems, where we distinguish:

- macrologistic systems – these include global economic processes taking place on the scale of a state, international organization, or transnational corporation. The obvious result of the macrologistic system is the logistics infrastructure in the form of communication routes, communication systems or sea, land, and airports,
- micrologistic systems – these refer to the logistics of an enterprise and processes related primarily to supply and supply of materials and raw materials, warehousing and storage of goods, production, services, sale, and distribution of products. Micrologistic systems are the basis for the existence (construction) of macrologistic systems,
- metalogistic systems – these are intermediate systems between macrologistic and micrologistic systems. They cover a large number of enterprises and the processes taking place between them. In other words, metalogistic systems are created by micrologistic systems working together.

A characteristic feature of the logistics systems listed above is that (Barcik & Jakubiec, 2011):

- the processes taking place in them, and related to movement (flow) and storage, overlap each other,
- in each of the systems, two spheres can be distinguished, respectively: the sphere of physical flows and the sphere of regulation.

In conclusion, it should be stated that during our lifetime we deal with a huge number of logistics systems. Understanding the specifics of their functioning, even of one, will allow us to understand all the others, including the more complex ones. In order to – in the theoretical part – make it easier to understand the essence of the functioning of the logistics system, we can use an example related to wine production. One of the supply chains is initiated at the time of opencast mining of quartz sand (glass sand), which is the basic ingredient for the production of glass. In this way, a glass bottle is produced. A second supply chain is initiated at the winery, where the winemaker plants the appropriate grape varieties and then harvests them and produces wine from them. Both chains connect in the bottling plant, where wine is poured into glass bottles, which then go onto storage shelves. The analysis of this simple case allows us to see important links in the integrated supply chain (see Figure 3.7). Each of the stages that make up the production of wine is important for the final result. In other words, by linking different supply chains, the entire system is physically merged. Because supply chains are often larger and more extensive, there will be more logistics systems and they will be more complex. And this means that they will be subject to further classifications. Nowadays, it is impossible to achieve market success without achieving success in supply chain management.[5] At this point, it is important to add that the enterprises, which make up the supply chain, are in fact interconnected through a network of physical flows and flows of information. According to Handfield (2020):

- physical flows include the transformation, movement, and storage of goods and materials. In addition, they are the most visible element of the supply chain, and equally important as the flow of information,
- information flows allow different business partners in the supply chain to coordinate their long-term plans and control the current flow of goods and materials, both up and down the supply chain.

2.2. Logistics audit, as an example of an industry audit

There is no doubt that the environment of the organization, especially over the last decade of the 20th century, has become more turbulent and therefore more difficult to predict. The increase in the intensity of changes is dictated primarily by the megatrends[6] related to the development of Industry 4.0 (see Section 2.5) and the threats posed to the global economy by the COVID-19 pandemic. Consequently, these circumstances strongly affect the processes of production, consumption, and investment that take place in many enterprises, as well as the social interactions that are the basic element of the functioning of people and nations. This makes it more difficult to run businesses effectively, which is often associated with maintaining a relatively high level of competitiveness in relation to other market players. That is why, much more often than even a decade ago, management staff reaches for audit as a tool for improving management systems and organizational processes. In practice, it is a source of knowledge about the state of functioning of a given organizational unit in terms of operations, finance, communication, security, or all activities carried out.

Nevertheless, better results are achieved by an audit that is adapted to the specifics of a given industry, including the essence and nature of the processes taking place in it. Hence the rapid increase in the popularity of the so-called industry audits. Jezierski (2007a) argues that industry audits are a source of important information on the condition and effectiveness of a given internal unit of the enterprise. An additional function of industry audits is to disseminate proper control along with the promotion of good changes and patterns and to maintain an optimal level of costs. What is important, in the opinion of Jezierski (2007a), is that industry audits are also a tool used to assess (often critically) the activities of the management staff and individual decision-making links of the organization. In other words, their main task is to provide information necessary for the continuous improvement of processes and systems related to the functioning of a given area and/or organizational unit within a given enterprise. An example of an industry audit is the logistics audit (a type of audit according to its subject – see Table 2.1). Its growing popularity is also the result of – in addition to the previously mentioned phenomena – the interest of enterprises in logistics and the increasingly frequent separation of logistics processes in organizations, which are not only becoming more complex but also play an increasingly important role in the enterprise operations. Hence, as Dendera-Gruszka et al. (2017) rightly point out, the logistics audit has developed as a tool for supervising and controlling logistics processes. Although "logistics audit" is still a relatively new term, the multiplicity of its definitional approaches in the literature on the subject may be surprising. Thus, according to the definition

Table 2.1 Basic objectives of logistics audit

Objectives of the logistics audit:
• Diagnosis of the state of logistics, the logistics system of the organization
• Identification of weaknesses and the possibility of improving the effectiveness of elements forming the organization's logistics system
• Elimination of errors in order to increase the quality of logistics services offered
• Development and implementation of logistic support conditions that will guarantee the continuous achievement of the highest quality of products and/or services
• Identifying opportunities to improve logistics activities in order to meet the requirements and expectations of customers
• Maintaining high quality and efficiency in the process of managing logistics processes
• Gaining the customer's trust in the quality of services and/or products offered, and the level of services provided, in order to increase the likelihood of maintaining constant cooperation with the client
• Ensuring proper relations with the internal and external environment of the organization
• Verification of risk factors affecting the quality of services provided and the costs of the organization's operation
• Accelerating and increasing flows in the logistics system
• Rationalization of logistics costs
• Improvement of operational activities along with optimization of the use of logistics
• Determination of the contribution and effects related to the cyclical conduct of a logistics audit

Source: Authors' own study based on Dendera-Gruszka et al. 2017, p. 26; Żebrucki, 2012, p. 425.

proposed by Klein (2018), a logistics audit analyzes and optimizes – step by step – the overall performance of the enterprise at various operational levels and increases the efficiency of the processes taking place. In addition, it removes bottlenecks that occur in operational processes through the implementation of restructuring activities. As a consequence, the level of service and the quality of logistics increase and logistics areas can be optimally used. Therefore, according to Klein, a logistics audit is the first step to a sustainable improvement in efficiency of the enterprise's operations. Similarly, although more concisely, the same concept is defined by Wawrzynowicz and Wajszczuk (2012), who state that a logistics audit is a systematic and independent analysis aimed at determining whether the activities regarding the quality of the logistics system and their results are consistent with the assumptions. An even simpler definition is proposed by Klug (2018), for whom a logistics audit is a systematic and independent control that diagnoses the logistics system of suppliers or contractors.[7] Žofková and Drábek (2019) also propose a broad approach to the term of logistics audit, stating that a logistics audit simply is a method of comprehensive and independent diagnosis of the enterprise's logistics system. A common feature that binds all the definitions of logistics audit mentioned above is that this audit refers primarily to the verification and then improvement of the logistics system functioning in a given enterprise. In other words, it can be said that a logistics audit is a tool used to check and analyze the discrepancies that occur in the operation of enterprise logistics systems, seeking differences between the declared and the actual state. At this point, however, it should be noted that a logistics audit is about the functioning of logistics systems of enterprises that are located and conduct their activities on different markets, in different sectors and industries. Thus, the specificity of a logistics audit cannot be identified with the TSL sector (transport – shipping – logistics) alone, or with logistics, but it should be treated much more broadly, going beyond the boundaries of the areas of activity listed here. In practice, a logistics audit is an activity that is aimed at achieving three basic objectives (for more, see Table 2.1):

- comparison of the actual state with the declared state (template) in the context of the functioning of the enterprise's logistics system,
- identification and analysis of deviations and dysfunctions occurring within the logistics system,
- providing recommendations and defining areas for improvement in order to eliminate anomalies.

All the presented objectives, in synthetic terms, can be reduced to an objective examination of existing operational processes and logistics flows, and then – on the basis of the collected information – provide recommendations and guidelines on how the logistics system (including logistics processes)

Table 2.2 Processes and areas subject to logistics audit

Processes subject to logistics audit	Areas subject to logistics audit
Warehousing	• Organization of warehouse space • Monitoring of warehousing process • Freight flows • Information flows • Intra-warehouse transfers • Warehouse infrastructure • Warehouse security • Technologies used • Security of information systems • Picking and preparation of orders • Inventory • Optimization of storage • Location of materials, goods, finished products, etc. • Competences of the staff handling warehouse processes • Personnel management • Identification of underlying issues • Warehouse releases • Release checks • Directions of improvement
Transport	• Organization of transport • Correctness of rolling stock selection • Evaluation of route planning • Efficiency of the rolling stock used • The right choice of transport (own/external transport) • Rolling stock replacement policy • Directions of improvement
Procurement	• Supplier classification analysis • Verification of supplier rating classification • Quality of service • Accuracy of providing offer information • Level of customer service • Supplier relations • Communication between individual links • Information flow • Delivery time • Speed of reaction and action • Ability to take emergency actions • Providing full information about the status of the order • Response and action in the event of a complaint or return • Verification of compliance of deliveries with the order

(Continued)

Table 2.2 (Continued)

Processes subject to logistics audit	Areas subject to logistics audit
Distribution	• Network configuration • Verification and identification of distribution channels • Level of integration of distribution channels • Dependency of supporting processes • Freight flows • Distribution organization • Analysis of network strengths and weaknesses • Directions of improvement
Inventory management	• Inventory structure • Stock size • Replenishment process • Inventory rotation • Directions of improvement
Order fulfillment	• Order fulfillment process • Order structure • Customer service • Customer service evaluation • Complaint and return process • Costs of order handling • Directions of improvement
Production	• Structure of the production process • Verification of production orders • Quality of manufactured products • Information flow • Speed of operation • Production plan • Accuracy and employee engagement • Employee competences • Quality and detail of technological documentation • Verification of production downtime • Control of the use of machinery and equipment • Freight flows • Production automation • Machine park replacement policy • Post-production control • Production costs • Process optimization • Innovation of production tools • Operation of machinery and equipment • Maintenance • Management of repairs and maintenance of machines and equipment • Quality of corrective actions • Production reports • Directions of improvement

(*Continued*)

Table 2.2 (Continued)

Processes subject to logistics audit	Areas subject to logistics audit
Supply Chain	• Process optimization • Direction of development of supply-chain activities • Verification of the condition of chain links • Supply-chain configuration • Use of infrastructure • Relationships between links • Communication between individual links • Resource flow • Use of modern technologies • Flexibility of operation • Response time to changes • Security of the information flow system • Verification of chain strengths and weaknesses • Directions of improvement
Packaging and secondary raw materials	• Identification and matching of packaging • Operation of packaging • Classification and management of packaging • Packaging recording • Method of recycling and recovery • Storage conditions • Directions of improvement

Source: (Dendera-Gruszka et al., 2017, p. 29).

or supply chain functions for a specific enterprise. In practice, the number of processes or, more generally, areas that can be subject to a logistic audit, is quite significant and concerns a wide range of activities that are carried out as part of the functioning of a given enterprise. In this context, the performance of activities related to logistics audit, even in the area of warehousing, consumes a notable amount of time, because the number of elements that must be tested is large. Table 2.2 presents in detail both the processes and the areas (including individual components) that are subject to a logistics audit within the enterprise.

Often, after a logistics audit has been carried out, a situation occurs in which a process has to be changed or improved so significantly that it is necessary to implement additional procedures and/or update existing ones. Thanks to this, enterprise managers have a detailed description of the procedure that should be followed when performing repetitive activities that will ultimately contribute to the achievement of the intended goals set within the framework of the enterprise's strategy adopted by the management board. Thus, as will be discussed in more detail, an effective logistics audit requires a high level of knowledge about the concepts, methods, techniques, and tools that will serve to improve the productivity of logistics processes.

2.3. Logistic audit – organization, stages, procedures

The organization and conduct of work related to the implementation of a logistics audit in an enterprise requires a sequence of activities that will make the implementation of the audit possible. On the other hand, efficiency in conducting a logistics audit will, in fact, be the result of two variables – the already-mentioned organization in its preparation, as well as knowledge about the areas that will be the subject of the auditor's research. This efficiency should be interpreted here as the possibility of a logistic audit to achieve the goal assigned to it. In the case of this type of audit, its general objective is – as already mentioned in Section 2.2 – to assess the state of the enterprise's logistics on an ongoing basis and to recommend measures aimed at improving the logistics processes functioning in the enterprise. Moreover, a successful logistics audit is inextricably linked to understanding the key stakeholders (including suppliers, business partners, customers, and local authorities) who directly or indirectly affect the logistics of the enterprise in general and its logistics system in particular. This means that, in practice, the requirements for auditors dealing with logistics audit should be, above all, good knowledge of issues related to broadly understood logistics, supply chain and logistics systems, as well as (preferably) several years of experience working in the logistics industry. Thus, in the opinion of the authors, this requirement should not be fulfilled by an auditor who has experience in the implementation of industry audits but not in those directly related to logistics; especially since industry audits, in comparison with, for example, financial audits, are characterized by a much higher degree of complexity, and thus of various problems. Each logistics audit should, therefore, be strictly tailored to the specific needs and requirements of each organization, and its initiation should be preceded by a thorough analysis and good preparation in the areas of:

- logistics audit planning – the plan and activities related to the implementation of the audit should be prepared in accordance with applicable standards and well in advance,
- research and critical analysis of existing data – auditors should have at their disposal relevant data, of high quality, coming from the organization (including its systems, processes, procedures, or from the employees themselves), which should then be subjected to detailed analysis. Only data prepared in this way should be compiled and compared with the adopted criteria and standards in order to formulate final conclusions and issue recommendations,
- communication – the results of the logistics audit should be clearly communicated to people who are directly and indirectly interested in

it. On the other hand, reporting methods, including post-audit reports, must comply with the applicable standards issued by the IIA,

- monitoring – logistics auditors should observe and control the functioning of the enterprise's logistics system or its supply chain on an ongoing basis in order to take corrective actions resulting from the completed logistics audit.

The next stage of preparatory work as part of the implementation of a logistics audit should include activities related to the construction and understanding of the logistics system model functioning within the analyzed enterprise. In practice this centers on (Gattorna et al., 1991):

a. defining the logistics goals of the enterprise in the context of broader corporate and marketing goals,
b. determining the target level of service provision and other logistics activities and products,
c. identifying flowcharts regarding communication in the execution of orders from customers,
d. identifying flowcharts of material flows and the corresponding data and information flows,
e. determining the places where there are discrepancies and overlapping flows of physical goods or information,
f. defining important interdependencies between the logistics function and other areas of activity.

Thanks to the analysis and graphical approach to the logistics system, the auditor will be able to know to what extent the processes existing within a given model achieve the goal assigned to them.

With knowledge of what prompts enterprises to conduct logistics audits and what actions, and in which areas these must be taken in this regard, we can now proceed to describe the basic stages of logistics audit implementation (see Table 2.3). The first stage focuses on the comprehensive preparation of the logistics audit and determining the principles under which it will be carried out. In practice, this is a series of activities that focus on determining the needs of the organization in the field of logistics audit, appointing a team of auditors (or auditor) and appointing the lead auditor (team leader), defining the main processes and those supporting the implementation of the enterprise's operational and strategic goals, determining the scope and scale of management involvement in the audit process, developing research areas, and informing employees about the date and rules for the implementation of audit activities. Often, the quality of the implementation of tasks resulting from the first stage of the logistics

Table 2.3 Basic stages of logistics audit implementation

Stages of logistics audit	Tasks
Stage I: Preparation of a holistic logistics audit concept	1.1. Prerequisites and motivation for conducting a logistic audit 1.2. Definition of the general objective and sub-objectives of the audit 1.3. Selection of auditors and possibly conclusion of an agreement with the entity 1.4. Involvement of management and use of their potential 1.5. Definition of the scope of the tests 1.6. Informing employees about the implementation of the audit
Stage II: Implementation of pre-audit actions	2.1. Development of an auditorium survey 2.2. Preparation of the audit plan and program 2.3. Conducting preliminary research by means of an auditorium-based survey 2.4. Analysis of the auditorium survey – obtaining information *vs.* inference 2.5. Preparation of pre-audit reports 2.6. Organization of an information meeting
Stage III: Implementation of the audit	3.1. Adoption of criteria for the evaluation of the studied area, unit, department, etc. 3.2. Determination of the actual state of logistics activities 3.3. Determination of the state of declared logistics activity 3.4. Comparative analysis of factual and declared facts 3.5. Inference 3.6. Indication of improvement activities (corrections, advice, recommendations)
Stage IV: Implementation of post-audit actions	4.1. Assessment of the course of audit activities as part of the audit 4.2. Evaluation of the correctness and quality of the data collected 4.3. Preparation of audit results 4.4. Recommendations for further audit activities in the areas concerned 4.5. Monitoring of improvement activities 4.6. Organizing the closing meeting

Source: Authors' own study.

audit has a significant impact on the others. Thus, the auditor should treat with particular care issues related to informing employees about the implementation of the logistics audit, because its efficiency and effectiveness will depend on their attitude, commitment, and emotional approach. The second stage, in contrast to the first, is already associated with the need to carry out pre-audit tasks, i.e., those immediately preceding the implementation of the proper audit. They include preparation of an audit survey, an audit plan and program, conducting preliminary individual and group surveys by means of a questionnaire, analysis and development of conclusions from the conducted research, and informing the management of the entity about the results of pre-audit activities. The third stage of the logistics audit is extremely important, because it is here that the actual state of logistics activity is determined and compared with the declared state. It is at this stage that not only the enterprise, but above all the management team, which is responsible for its development, is informally evaluated for its previous work. The final product of this stage of logistics audit comes in the form of conclusions, corrections, and recommendations, which are then included in post-audit reports, which are the foundation of each audit's documentation. The fourth stage is the final one and in fact boils down to assessing both the course of audit activities and the correctness of the collected data and presenting the final results of the audit. At this stage, the auditor also formulates recommendations as to the need to undertake audit work in other areas of the organization in the future. A kind of overarching mechanism connecting the entire program and conduct of the logistics audit is the organization of the closing meeting, which is a holistic summary of the work related to the audit carried out in the enterprise. Table 2.3 presents a detailed list of tasks that are carried out at individual stages of the logistics audit.

In order to supplement knowledge about the stages of logistics audit, a block diagram of its implementation in graphic terms is presented (see Figure 2.2), which is to contribute to its better consolidation.

The logistics audit is increasingly being considered as an important tool for improving processes taking place in organizations because it takes up important topics from the point of view of the organization's management, concerned with assessing the quality of logistics operations, the level of productivity of logistics systems, or the effectiveness of managing relationships with customers and suppliers. Thanks to its use, management staff can make a deeper diagnosis of problem areas, for example by quickly identifying key deviations that may occur both within the existing logistics infrastructure, logistics organization, logistics system, supply chain, or ICT infrastructure. In this context, the question arises when and under what circumstances the enterprise management should use a logistics audit[8] and what measurable benefits it can bring him. The answer to this question is neither simple nor unambiguous, especially considering the set of specific features and problems that characterize each organization. However, while making a certain generalization, it can be said that the basic premises for implementing a logistics audit in an enterprise should be:

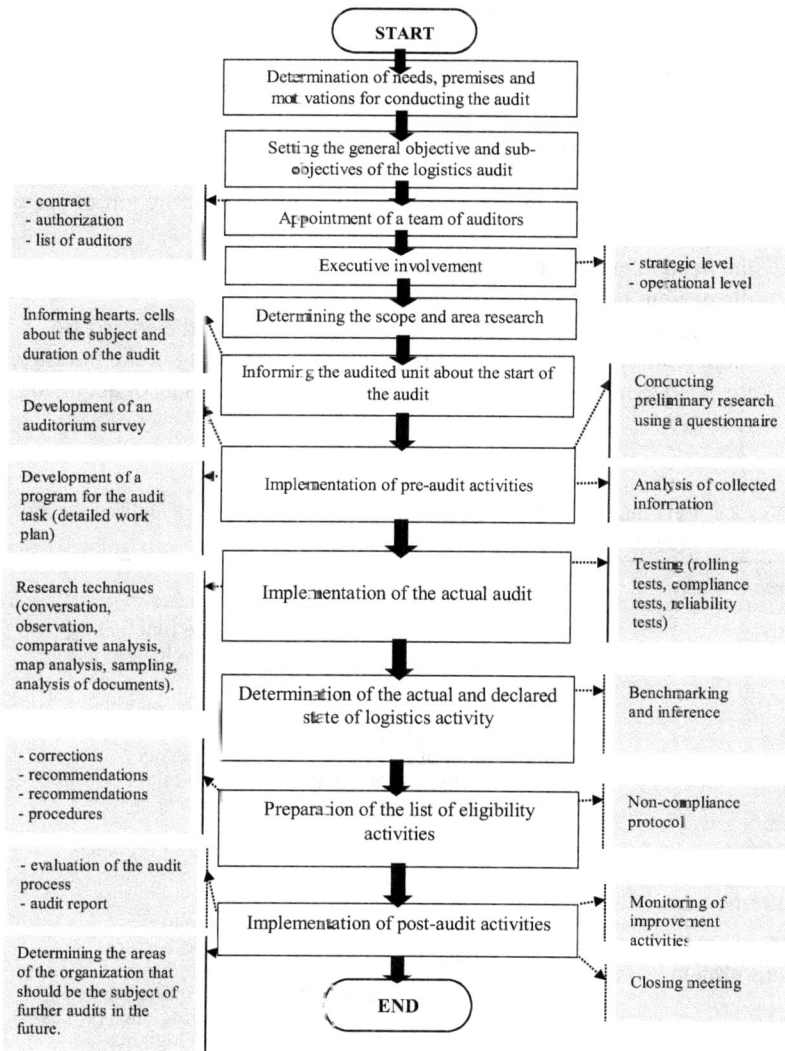

Figure 2.2 Logistics audit procedure – graphic design Source: Authors' own study.

- the need to verify the compliance of existing information on the results of logistics operations with reality,
- low or decreased work efficiency,
- the need to reduce the costs of warehouse, transport, and distribution logistics,
- the desire to improve the functioning of the supply chain,
- the need to improve key logistics parameters,
- implementation of an investment related to the construction of warehouse infrastructure,
- the need to automate processes,
- the need to optimize the adopted business strategy,
- a decrease in the level of market competitiveness of the enterprise,
- the intention to introduce best practices/benchmarking in the industry,[9]
- the need to measure enterprise value as a result of its sale or acquisition (merger).

Table 2.4 Benefits resulting from the implementation of logistics audit in the areas of processes, infrastructure, organization

Area	Benefits
Process	• Objective (independent) opinion on the functioning of logistics, logistics system, or supply chain in the organization • Optimization of purchasing, production, warehouse, and distribution processes • Automation of repetitive logistics processes • Streamlining complex logistics processes • Elimination of bottlenecks in the process • Standardization of procedures • Shortening the time of implementation of logistics processes
Infrastructure	• Optimization of product storage • Increasing safety processes in the warehouse • Overall improvement of logistics infrastructure
Organization	• Improving the quality of logistics data • Clearly defined responsibilities and responsibilities • Improving the efficiency of control of logistics processes • Increase in competences in the area of logistics • Quick assessment of the logistic potential of the organization by comparing with the best models • Estimation of the costs of logistics processes • Cost reduction • Reduction of risks related to the functioning of the organization • Reducing the burden of managing the entire organization • Increase in the return on assets

Source: Authors' own study.

As for the benefits that the enterprise can gain – incidentally on many levels – thanks to the use of an auxiliary tool in the form of a logistics audit, their list is significant and is presented in detail below in Table 2.4. On this basis, we can also conclude that the greatest asset for an enterprise using this type of audit is the ability to improve (enhance/perfect) the logistics system by identifying ineffective activities and agreeing on directions of improvement of processes, procedures, and systems in a specific area of the organization. As a consequence, there is both a reduction in the costs of logistics activities and an increase in the quality of services provided.

2.4. Problem areas of the logistics audit

According to Kaczmarek (2016), each organization is always characterized by a certain "organized complexity" and a system of interconnected sub-systems, the functioning and cooperation of which determine its existence and development. Since the organization remains in constant interactions, often multidimensional and dynamic, with its environment, it is natural that they can be a source of support and help, as well as obstacles or problems. In practice, in the process of managing the organization management staff constantly encounter some difficulties or dysfunctions, due to – holistically speaking – the permanent failure of the organization to adapt to the rapidly changing world, the matter of which is as interesting as it is unpredictable. Therefore, it can be concluded that problems are in fact an immanent feature of the functioning of any organization and a natural everyday reality for its managers.

At the beginning of the considerations on the problem areas of logistics audit, it is worth making a few remarks about the essence of the very concept of the problem, which – and this is worth emphasizing – in management science has received many interpretations, but not always ones enriching its content or essence. Nevertheless, the problem is most often understood as a difficulty that can take on a theoretical or practical character, and that causes an inquisitive attitude, leading ultimately to enrichment of knowledge (Kupisiewicz, 1964). A more comprehensive approach to the term is proposed by Nosal (1993), who believes that the problem becomes everything that raises our – even the slightest – doubt, causes discrepancies between the actual and expected state, and hinders the possibility of solving the task using available knowledge and developed methods (formulas). The concept is defined slightly differently by Linhart (1976), who believes that the problem is in practice an interactive relationship between the subject and its environment, having the features of internal conflict, which the subject tries to solve by seeking to move from the initial state to the final state (goal). According to Linhart, it is the existence of the problem itself that is in fact the source of motivation for the subject to solve it. At the same time, as he quickly adds, in order to solve a specific problem, the entity must look for new and often non-standard solutions that will go beyond the previously adopted framework. This is also associated with the need to search for new sources of knowledge and information on effective ways of solving problems or, more broadly, problem situations. Thus, summarizing the content contained in the above definitions of the word problem, we can conventionally assume that it is any situation (quantified or not) that requires a solution by a person or a group of people, using both standard and non-standard (read: new) means (patterns, tools, techniques, etc.). On the basis of science – including management science – problems can take both different forms, can be subject to non-uniform criteria of division, and be the subject of a wide range of research. Detailed information on this subject is included in Table 2.5, which comprehensively presents the types of problems faced by researchers, who undertake scientific research in various fields of knowledge and science.

Understanding the word problem – including its types, divisions, and references – means that we can now move on to discuss another, closely related issue concerning the "problem area." The answer to the question "what is a problem area," is neither easy nor unambiguous. This situation is caused by interpretative considerations, because the term itself in the literature of management science has been explained many times. Apart from this thread, however, we can assume that we will consider as problem areas in management those organizational and technical spheres of enterprise functioning that are the source of anomalies and deviations. Moreover, eliminating problem areas requires the involvement of forces and resources that may come from within the organization and/or from its external environment. At this point, it should be emphasized that in studies – not only those of a scientific nature – the term "problem area" is often used interchangeably with such terms as difficult areas, conflict areas, danger areas, areas of deviation, or – in general – research areas. However, the use of the term "research areas" seems to be the most appropriate, i.e., the closest to the term "problem areas," because from the point of view of the theory of logic, the solution of any conflict or problem should be preceded by a thorough analysis of its nature, and thus be well studied. Thus, problem areas are defined within various fields of science, scientific disciplines, or specialties. The result of this is scientific research conducted e.g., on problem areas in Poland, in the aspect of the objectives of the Regional Policy of the European Union (EU), problem areas of project management, or identification of problem areas in supply-chain management. Problem areas are also identified and then investigated as part of a logistics audit. Their distinction also requires the use of the right approach (diagnostic approach, prognostic

Table 2.5 Types of research problems – characteristics

Division criterion	Type of problem	Characteristics of the problem	Author/Source
Nature of the problem	Deviation problems	Problems related to the formation of various types of defects in the organization, the causes of which are not known to us. In order to eliminate these deviations, it is necessary to conduct studies that will determine their cause. However, the information collected during the research is to prevent the emergence of such problems in the future	Penc, 2007
	Optimization problems	Problems that arise as a result of the need to introduce adaptive changes in the current functioning of the organization, due to changes taking place in its closer and further environment. It is about improving management methods, processes, techniques, functions, tools, systems, logistics, information flow, etc., in order to improve the efficiency of the entire organization	
	Innovative problems	Problems resulting from creative changes taking place both in the organization and in its environment. Nowadays, innovation is seen as an important element of the organization's offensive strategy, especially those organizations entering new markets, as well as a defensive weapon for those that already have a stable market position and a good reputation	
Degree of structuring	Well-structured problems	Problems whose structure is well known to us mainly in quantitative terms. These problems can be quantified because they have been well recognized, and mathematical models and precise measurement tools have been developed to solve them	Antoszkiewicz, 1999

(Continued)

Table 2.5 (Continued)

Division criterion	Type of problem	Characteristics of the problem	Author/Source
	Poorly structured problems	Problems with a poorly defined structure. They contain both qualitative and quantitative elements. At the same time, the quality elements are the ones that stand out	
	Unstructured problems	Problems with an indefinite structure. They can be defined only qualitatively – in verbal form – due to the lack of quantitative relationships between the elements. These kinds of problems can be described, but they cannot be measured	
Complexity	Simple problems	Basic problems, usually the relationships between the elements of the problem are linear, so specific causes give rise to specific effects	Own elaboration
	Compound problems	Problems that are bigger than simple problems, usually the relationships between the elements of the problem are non-linear and can take on different forms or forms	
	Complex problems	Highly complex problems, often involving larger parts of the organization. These are problems whose effects are difficult to predict and their occurrence can give rise to a domino effect	
	Chaos problems	Crisis-based problems. Requiring quick intervention and action on the part of management	
Creation status	Problems related to the improvement of the existing state	These are problems regarding deviations and optimizations. The starting point for solving them is to determine the facts	Bielińska-Dusza, 2009
	Problems with creating a new organization	Problems related to the implementation of forecasts and long-term plans	

Source: Authors' own study.

approach), selecton of appropriate indicators (quantitative, qualitative), adoption of specific measurement scales (nominal scale, ordinal scale, interval scale, quotient scale), and the use of the appropriate inference scheme (deductive inference, inductive inference). To sum up, we can see that the proper diagnosis of a problem area requires not only knowledge and experience within a given sector or industry but also the ability to apply appropriate measurement techniques. Only then can the areas designated in this way be called problem areas. Taking into account the above, Lisiński (2011) distinguishes three basic groups of research problems as part of a logistics audit:

- first group – this involves the assessment of the appropriateness of the logistics strategy adopted by the organization to the strategy of the enterprise itself and the review and evaluation of the process of defining the logistics strategy.
- second group – this concerns the analysis and evaluation of solutions in the area of logistics organization, the location of logistics tasks in the organizational structure of the enterprise, and the ways of performing logistics functions,
- third group – this refers directly to the research and analysis of logistics processes taking place in the organization, and related to production logistics, supply logistics, distribution logistics, waste logistics, storage, transport, inventory, or IT systems.

It should be noted that the main problem (research) areas of logistics audit (see Bielińska-Dusza, 2009) presented by Lisiński (2011) in fact correspond to the basic areas of activity of each organization, concerning strategy, structure, and processes. In the case of processes, Table 2.6 below, presents – in an exhaustive manner – the characteristics of problem areas that are most often subjected to research and analysis as part of the implementation of tasks in the field of logistics audit. Thus, from the scale of effective identification of errors, deviations, anomalies, and irregularities in these areas (see Table 2.6), we will be able to talk about either healthy or pathological features of the system related to the functioning of the logistics system within a given enterprise.

2.5. Logistics audit in the era of Industry 4.0

There is no denying that, in fact, since the dawn of time, technological breakthroughs have brought about, and continue to do so, fundamental changes in economies and societies in almost every respect. In general, they

Table 2.6 Typology of problem areas of logistics audit

Area	Characteristics
Warehouse management	Its aim is to improve operational activities and optimize the use of warehouse equipment, organize and monitor the storage process, analyze goods and information flows in the storage process, and identify key problems of warehouse management
Inventory management	It covers the structure of inventories, their rotation coverage rate, the process of replenishment of stock, and directions of improvement
Order fulfillment	It concerns the structure of orders, the assessment of the costs of handling complaints and returns, as well as the examination of the level of handling complaints and returns and the actual level of customer service
Transport	It is related to the implementation of activities in the area of transport, the correctness of the selection of rolling stock, the efficiency of its use, the choice between own and foreign transport, rolling stock management, indicating the directions of improvements in this area
Logistic information systems	It includes analysis and assessment of the degree of implementation of information systems, determination of the use of individual information channels, analysis of document circulation, determination of network architecture, tests of existing hardware security, verification of the effectiveness of systems, ensuring security of access to systems
Packaging and recyclable resources	Diagnosis of packaging burdened with the obligation of recovery, determination of the method of their recording, the optimal way to ensure the required levels of recovery and recycling
Distribution system	It includes audits in the areas of warehousing, inventory management, transportation and order fulfillment, network configuration, freight flows, distribution organization and improvement directions
Production system	It involves a reliable assessment of production logistics and setting priorities enabling the right and effective decisions related to it; besides, it allows you to improve operational activities and optimize the use of the enterprise's production infrastructure. It covers all aspects of production, from planning sales cycles, through storage and supply of raw materials, flows on production halls, to production reporting with its marking
Supply system	It is subordinated to the review of the status of the procedures of the purchasing department and the verification of commercial contracts. This includes analysis of the ordering system, suppliers and prices, verification of contracts and preliminary preparation for negotiations with suppliers, as well as analysis and structure of inventory

(Continued)

Table 2.6 (Continued)

Area	Characteristics
Supply chain	It allows, among other things, the identification of the strengths and weaknesses of the chain and the processes implemented in it, analysis of the current configuration of the supply chain and the infrastructure used, and assessment of the relationship between the links
Cross-docking*	It allows for reducing total costs in the supply chain, thanks to the fact that the goods are not stored. However, the effective and effective use of cross-docking requires precise synchronization of processes related to the receipt and release of goods
Automation of logistics processes*	It concerns the implementation of a comprehensive solution that will integrate human resources, material resources (machines), and advanced IT systems. It can cover all areas of logistics audit. The scale of process automation should be economically justified and take into account the permissible level of errors in processes, the exceeding of which gives rise to significant levels of risk for the organization

Source: (Żebrucki, 2012, p. 427).
* Typology supplemented with areas added by the authors of the study.

take the form of technical, economic, and social transformations, which significantly transform the current picture of the functioning of the world both qualitatively and quantitatively. It is common to call such phenomena industrial revolutions[10] or, less frequently, industrial overthrows. The term Industrial Revolution was used for the first time at the end of the 18th century to describe the mechanization of production with the participation of steam and water (steam age), which gave rise to mechanical production systems. Then came the Second Industrial Revolution (at the end of the 19th century and the beginning of the 20th), which resulted in the construction of the world's first assembly line at the Ford automotive plant (in 1913). Subsequently, the key issues for the Second Industrial Revolution in the form of standardization and mechanization of production evolved toward its coordination and automation, which formed, in turn, the Third Industrial Revolution (1970s). However, in relation to its predecessors, it was already characterized by a high degree of automation of industrial production (the era of industrial automation), which, incidentally, was the result of the use of advanced information and communication systems. Nowadays, we are already dealing with the Fourth Industrial Revolution, the creation of which would not have been possible without the participation of advanced technology, in the form of the Internet. To a level previously unknown, it revolutionized the level of innovation of products, services, systems, or technologies available on the market. The latter have evolved from the digital level to the level of artificial intelligence (AI)[11] and machine learning (ML).[12] Moreover, the scope of the Fourth Industrial Revolution is much more extensive and much more profound than it was in earlier such phenomena (Buła & Niedzielski, 2021). Currently, not only based on theory but also practice, we use the term "Industry 4.0" much more often – referring to the current industrial revolution – rather than the "fourth industrial revolution." Nevertheless, both these terms function in public space as synonyms[13] and are therefore used interchangeably. Industry 4.0 – as a conceptual category – has functioned in the world of science and business since 2011 thanks to the annual industrial trade show Hannover Messe. The use of the phrase "Industry 4.0" was directly related to the concept of "Industrie 4.0," promoted by the representatives of the German business, political, and scientific world in favor of strengthening the competitiveness of German industry, in the face of quickly catching up on competition from China. As a result, the development of Industry 4.0 has become a key element in Germany's new research and technological innovation policy. This idea was rapidly taken up by the governments of other countries, especially those that want to maintain their good market position on the map of global competitiveness. As for the objectives that guide the idea of Industry 4.0, they relate primarily to (Hochmuth et al., 2017):

1) At the level of strategy:
   a) building new business models and services using digital products,
   b) shortening the time of introducing new products to the market, in response to rapidly changing customer requirements,
   c) increasing the degree of resistance of the organization to changing customer tastes,
2) At the level of the organization:
   a) improving the quality of work by better reconciling professional and private duties,
   b) automation of routine tasks,
   c) creating a user-oriented work environment thanks to innovative human–machine interaction,
3) At process level:
   a) time savings due to more efficient and transparent production processes,
   b) increasing the flexibility of processes through dynamic planning, control, and execution,
   c) increase productivity and save resources for customized products,
   d) shortening the time of process implementation using intelligent analyses,

e) diversification of work organization through mobile control and execution processes,
f) increase quality by predictively avoiding errors,
g) increase the efficiency of processes using technology in the areas of data collection, data transfer, and data analysis.

In the context of the above-mentioned objectives, therefore, the question arises: what are they supposed to serve? The answer – which may be surprising – is not difficult, because in the era of Industry 4.0, a completely new model of organization (enterprises, factories) will be developed, which – unlike its predecessors – will be "smarter" (see Table 2.7). The combination of the adjective "intelligent" with the noun "factory" is by no means accidental, because the point is that the newly formed type of organization should act similarly to a thinking being and adapt its functioning to the changing environment through appropriate adaptation of the most modern solutions and technologies.

In practice, smart factories are therefore to become enterprises based on cyber-physical systems and linking them with the use of the Internet of Things in industry and organization of production.[14] The structure that will connect all the devices, sensors, systems, and machines in the enterprise will cause production losses, malfunctions, and downtime to disappear. In addition, goods produced in smart factories will be characterized by a high level of customization, and production processes will be characterized by a high level of digitization.

Highly advanced technology related to Industry 4.0 (including the Internet of Things, Internet of Services, cyber-physical systems) will therefore also significantly determine the future shape, "appearance," and structure of the internal audit, which is already referred to as the "fourth generation internal audit" (Internal Audit 4.0, IA 4.0). Its final face is not yet known to us, but there is no doubt that Internal Audit 4.0 (like Logistics Audit 4.0) will be a process of objective acquisition of data from the Internet, cyber-physical systems, and factories of the future, which, subjected to analysis and model visualization, will identify patterns, anomalies, or deviations from the desired state. Thanks to this, internal auditors will be able to carry out the tasks they face more effectively than before, which in practice will bring enterprises closer to achieving their goals at both the operational and strategic levels. There is no doubt that smart factories will need a "smart" audit that is tailored to their structures, tools, processes, and strategies. Thus, it can be expected that auditing as we know it today will evolve toward digital audit (see Table 2.8) – this also applies to industry audits, including logistics audit – mainly due to the undeniable fact that the world itself is becoming more digital (for more on this, see Section 1.3)

Table 2.7 Modern enterprise *vs.* future enterprise – similarities and differences

Item	Data Source	Contemporary enterprise		The enterprise of the future	
		Features	Technology	Features	Technology
Tool	Sensor	Precision	Intelligent sensors and fault detection	Self-awareness, self-assessment	Monitoring degradation, predicting the remaining service life
Machine	Controller	Efficiency, productivity	Monitoring and diagnostics of equipment operating conditions	Self-awareness, self-assessment, self-resistance	Uptime with predictive "health" monitoring
Production system	Network system	Productivity and overall equipment efficiency	Cost-effective operations: reduction of labor and waste	Self-employment, self-configuration, self-organization	Hassle-free productivity

Source: Lee et al. (2015).

Table 2.8 Changes taking place in internal audit

Area	Historical	Contemporary	Innovative
Purpose	Audit of units carried out on a rotational basis, or the basis of an approved plan	Audit of units carried out on the basis of defined risk areas	Audit of units based on strategic, operational and business risk
Perspective	Historical	Historical	Future-oriented
Style	Corporate	Patriarchal	Consultative, advisory, and expert
Authorization	Compliance with policies and procedures	Ensuring financial control: compliance	Business compliance
Focus on risk	Financial	Financial	Corporate
Toolbox	Abacus, calculators	IT programs to provide control for key processes	Highly advanced digital tools using artificial intelligence and machine-learning technology
Technology	Basic office supplies	Automated working documents	Digital testing and continuous monitoring

Source: Authors' own study based on (Norman, 2009, p. 10).

This situation is likely to herald a turnaround in the internal audit over the next few years, due to the rapid digitization of enterprises and institutions. Its scope will cover almost the entire methodology of conducting internal audit, including, in particular, audit tools and techniques. The changes will concern in particular:

- The method of collecting, preparing, and analyzing data – at this point it should be mentioned that thanks to such technologies as cloud computing, big data, the Internet of Things (IoT), etc., it will be possible to access data (information) in real time from anywhere in the world. This means that auditors will not have to – as has been the case so far – waste a lot of time gaining access to these technologies, which has often been difficult for reasons such as logistics. In addition, the entire process related to the processing of audit data will be digitized, which means that basic and even advanced audit tasks in applications or data sources will no longer require human intervention, but only supervision. Technologically advanced solutions will also allow auditors to extract the right information even from those data sets that are not structured (e.g., images, sounds, videos, posts, text files, emails). What's more, the new solutions will allow for better identification of risk in the organization, using tools that will combine elements of statistics, data visualization, data and process mining, artificial intelligence, machine learning, or algorithmics,

- control and security of information in various areas of the organization – due to the fact that digital data are most often stored in IT systems or databases, access to them will be granted and supervised by machines based on algorithms. In practice, this is to prevent an attempt to misuse them by unauthorized persons,
- The basic scope of knowledge, competences, and skills – because organizations, and thus internal audit, will undergo far-reaching digitization, it will be necessary to supplement the specialist knowledge in the audit with new elements, related to, for example, computer science or algorithmics. Nevertheless, the human factor will remain the most important value for the enterprise, as the ultimate guarantor of the validity and quality of the audit process in both holistic and fragmented terms. However, in the case of competences and skills, cognitive abilities[15] and meta-skills[16] will play a special role among auditors and employees.

2.6.   Control and analytical questions

Control questions

1. Give a definition and briefly characterize the logistics system of the enterprise.
2. Give a definition – broadly and narrowly – of a logistics audit.
3. Present the basic goals that a logistics audit has to achieve.
4. The areas subject to logistic audit in storage and production processes are …?
5. Complete the basic stages – along with the tasks assigned to them – of the logistics audit.
6. Present in a graphical terms the procedure for the course of a logistics audit.
7. Describe the benefits of a logistics audit in the areas of processes and organizations.
8. Characterize the problem area of logistics audit in relation to warehouse management, production systems, and automation of logistics processes.
9. According to Lisiński (2011), as part of the logistics audit, there are three basic groups of research problems. What are they?

10. Describe the changes taking place in the internal audit, taking into account the area related to the purpose of the audit, the style, and the technology used.

Analytical questions

1. In the opinion of Jezierski (2007a), industry audits are a tool used to assess the activities of management and individual decision-making links of the organization, and their main task is to provide information necessary for continuous improvement of processes and systems related to the functioning of a given area and/or organizational unit within a given enterprise. With that in mind, do you agree that industry audits will continue to grow in popularity over the next few years? Justify your opinion.
2. Since the logistics audit is a voluntary audit and therefore carried out at the request of the ordering party, under what circumstances would you recommend – to the management of the organization – its conduct?
3. What benefits and disadvantages do you see from the implementation of a logistics audit at the strategic and operational level of the organization?
4. On the basis of science and practice, the phrase "the world in which we live is becoming more and more digital" is more and more often repeated. In your opinion, does this mean that logistics auditing is also becoming more and more a digital audit? Give your opinion on this topic using practical examples.
5. Describe possible scenarios for the development of logistics audit in the context of Industry 4.0.

Notes

1 The founder of general systems theory is considered to be the Austrian biologist and philosopher Ludwig von Bertalanffy, who interpreted the system as a whole consisting of parts remaining in a state of interaction. For more information, see Von Bertalanffy L. (1984) *General Systems Theory: Basics, Development, Applications*, PWN, Warsaw.

2 Nevertheless, we should be aware that the concept of a system is defined differently depending on the area in which it is applied. Therefore, in the opinion of Szklarski and Kozioł (1980), it can take on different meanings and, in technology, the system is understood as assigning to a specific purpose the operation of a set of objects interconnected with each other; in organization and planning, the system is understood as a set of time-related operations; in scientific and research work, the system is understood as the field of general methodology for the study of processes and phenomena related to any area of human activity;

while in the field of cognitive theory, the system means a certain method of scientific thinking in the process of solving complex control tasks.

3 For more information, see https://www.elalog.eu/.

4 According to Gołembska (2010) elements of the logistics system are material and human resources, as well as source data and information that can be separated into homogeneous logistics subsystems, are fully reflected in the enterprise's financial documentation, and are a quantitatively and quantitatively record of the volume and structure of demand for products or services.

5 This is the active management of supply-chain activities that aims to maximize customer value and achieve a sustainable competitive advantage. In practice, this induces enterprises to run and develop your supply chains in the most efficient way. Activities in this area include product development, procurement, production, distribution, and IT systems, which are currently necessary to coordinate these activities.

6 For more on the impact of megatrends on the global economy and societies, see Naisbitt, J. (1997). *Megatrends: Ten New Directions Changing Our Lives*. Zysk i S-ka Wydawnictwo, Poznań.

7 An example of a narrow approach to the definition of logistics audit can be that proposed by Sungurtekin (2011), for whom a logistics audit is an activity that always begins with the collection of quantitative and qualitative data from key stakeholders of the organization and their analysis and interpretation. On the other hand, the main units cooperating and participating in the collection of this data and conducting interviews are most often the following departments: logistics, transport, warehouse, purchasing, production, trade, customer service, or IT. All of them are directly or indirectly involved in the supply chain and can provide valuable insights into the situation and benefit from the results and conclusions contained in the documentation post-auction.

8 A logistics audit is a voluntary audit. This means that it is carried out at the request of the ordering party and it is not the result of the law.

9 The process of improvement, consisting of the use of experience and the best global models and practices that are implemented for the needs of the organization.

10 It is widely believed that we can talk about an industrial revolution when there is a significant increase in the efficiency of production systems, which is the result of the use of new technology.

11 Artificial intelligence is, in fact, a specific type of system that can rationally solve multidimensional problems or take actions to achieve previously set goals. The term "artificial intelligence" was first used in 1955 by the eminent mathematician and computer scientist John McCarthy.

12 Machine learning is an area of artificial intelligence concerning algorithms that participate in the process of self-improvement through their experience. In other words, it is a process in which the computer learns something new on its own, based on algorithms and collected data.

13 There are also other synonyms for the term "Industry 4.0" in the literature, including Industry of the Future, The Cyber-Physical System Era (CPSs Era), Production of the Future, Intelligent manufacturing systems (IMSs), and 4IR (Fourth Industrial Revolution). In Anglo-Saxon countries, the term "Internet of Things" is also used, as is the "Internet of Everything" (IoE) and the "Industrial Internet of Things" (IIoT).

14 This is a prediction by specialists (Robinson, J. (2014). *Smart Factory and the Internet of The Things Opportunity*. https://blogs.intel.com/) who claim that by 2025, 80 to 100 percent of production may already be using applications for Internet stuff. This means that machines, sensors, and other devices will connect to each other and communicate via the Internet.

15 Cognitive abilities include thinking, speech, evaluating, understanding, data processing, and spatial orientation.

16 These are abilities that allow an individual to function effectively in a rapidly changing reality or environment.

3 Logistics audit

A modular approach

3.1. Logistics audit of procurement

Synchronization and communication of processes related to materials management are among the most difficult activities that logisticians have to perform in order for the supply subsystem in the enterprise's logistics system to function properly. In terms of definition, materials management concerns those spheres of economic activity that cover all phenomena and processes related to the management of materials[1] (raw materials, semi-finished products) at all levels of management (Statistics Poland, 2020). The processes taking place in the area of materials management include those that relate to the acquisition, supply, and use of materials in all phases of the economic process and their movement (delivery). A complementary – although slightly different – view of the essence of material management in the enterprise is presented by J. Arnold et al. (2008), who claim that it performs a coordinating function both in terms of planning and of controlling the flow of materials in the organization. At the same time, they point to the implementation of two basic goals, which are reduced to:

- maximizing the use of the limited resources of the organization,
- providing the required level of customer service.

Let us note that the objectives presented within the framework of material management, although they are equivalent to each other, nevertheless contain a certain element of antinomicity. In practice, it is not easy to provide customers with what they want, taking into account the limitations that often result from time and space, while maintaining low costs. And this means that materials management must be a compromise between the level of customer service and the cost of services provided to them. Especially since these costs increase in direct proportion to the level and quality of what is offered. Due to this, alternative solutions are constantly

DOI: 10.4324/9781003380184-4

being sought based on practice, which, thanks to the potential savings made in various areas of the enterprise's operations, will compensate for the costs it incurs in the field of customer service. Thus, one should agree with the thesis put forward by Arnold et al. (2008) that the general problem of materials management is that of maintaining a balance between priority and efficiency. In the context of materials management, the priority for the organization still remains the importance with which it approaches production planning in relation to market demand, which is determined by the volume of demand. In the case of efficiency, it is primarily about the most effective functioning of the organization's operating system, which will be a determinant in the context of the volume of production or goods delivered to the market. Both the first and the second conceptual categories referred to here must be subject to constant verification and control in order to be able to effectively meet the requirements set for them by customers who constantly demand better prices and higher quality of service. These challenges must be faced by materials management on a daily basis. Nowadays – especially in the field of logistics – next to materials management, the element that can ultimately determine the success or failure of the enterprise is procurement. According to Słowiński (2008), it is a concept that has a broader meaning than purchasing,[2] and should be understood as a process of acquiring goods and services. As he quickly adds, procurement is a process that deliberately connects the participants in the supply chain and guarantees the right quality that is provided by the suppliers in this chain. The cardinal task of a well-functioning procurement process is to ensure that the raw materials and semi-finished products necessary in the production process are delivered when they are needed. In addition, the enterprise's logistics system has several other tasks to fulfill (Lysons, 2004):

- the purchase of materials necessary for production on the basis of its plan,
- the organization of the flow of information and financial resources regarding the purchase of materials,
- verifying that the material in question is of sufficiently good quality,
- identification of new suppliers and establishing close cooperation with them,
- negotiating prices from suppliers and conditions for the purchase of raw materials,
- control of deliveries,
- finalizing deliveries,
- receipt and storage of deliveries,
- maintaining a low (optimal) level of stocks,

- close integration and cooperation with departments using the purchased materials, taking into account understanding their needs and obtaining materials at the right time.

In relation to the tasks described above, that are to be accomplished by the sphere of procurement in the functioning of the enterprise, it should be emphasized only that its economic effectiveness – in a holistic approach – will not be determined only by the fact of obtaining raw materials for production at the lowest possible price but by the synergy effect that it can achieve from cooperation in the implementation of each of the tasks. The last element, next to materials management and procurement, which in the context of a logistics audit of procurement needs to be discussed, is the so-called procurement logistics. In terms of the explanatory approach, procurement logistics is a process that determines the distribution, condition, and flows of materials in an enterprise and requires constant coordination (Krawczyk, 2000). As noted by Skuza (2019), its main role is to prevent a situation in which production could be interrupted. Therefore, it must effectively and economically meet all the materials needs that the enterprise has. In practice, this boils down to the fact that procurement logistics must simultaneously ensure the expected completeness, reliability, and quality of deliveries on the one hand, and guarantee their timeliness, flexibility, and speed on the other. Any disturbances in this area may hinder, or even prevent, the proper functioning of the entire logistics system of the enterprise. This is because the system is characterized by a high degree of consistency, which consequently leads to a situation where changes made within one subsystem mechanically imply those occurring in others. As Mroczko (2016) emphasizes, procurement logistics is therefore a complicated process, especially since it must strive to minimize the costs associated with the purchase and maintenance of inventory, as well as to maintain their high quality. What seems to distinguish procurement logistics from other elements of the enterprise's logistics system is that it is strongly connected with the market because all the materials necessary to secure the production process come from the market. Thus, it is a key link in the supply chain of any enterprise. In synthetic terms, the main goal that procurement logistics has to achieve is considered to be (Kowalczyk, 2015):

- obtaining from the market and preparing materials for production,
- organizing an efficient flow of materials and information assigned to it.

Its implementation is the result of tasks and activities, which in graphic terms are presented in Figure 3.1.

Tasks	Actions	
Ensuring optimal product quality	- selection of the right supplier - negotiations on quality - control of deliveries	
Minimization of total costs	- make or buy decision - negotiation of other conditionals, that determine the level of costs	
Acquiring and retaining reliable and competitive suppliers	- analysis of the supply market - evaluation and selection of the supplier - strategic building relations with suppliers - conclusion and performance of contracts - action to improve the image enterprises among suppliers	Procurement logistics objectives
Minimum stock level and smooth flow of raw materials	- planning of material needs - decision on supply size, frequency - organizing he flow of raw materials - component management supply - internal transport - organizing the procurement process	
Cooperation and integration with other areas of the enterprise	- planning needs on the basis of production and sales schedule - organizing an efficient flow of materials for the first station on the production line - information flow management - financial planning when buying high-value materials	

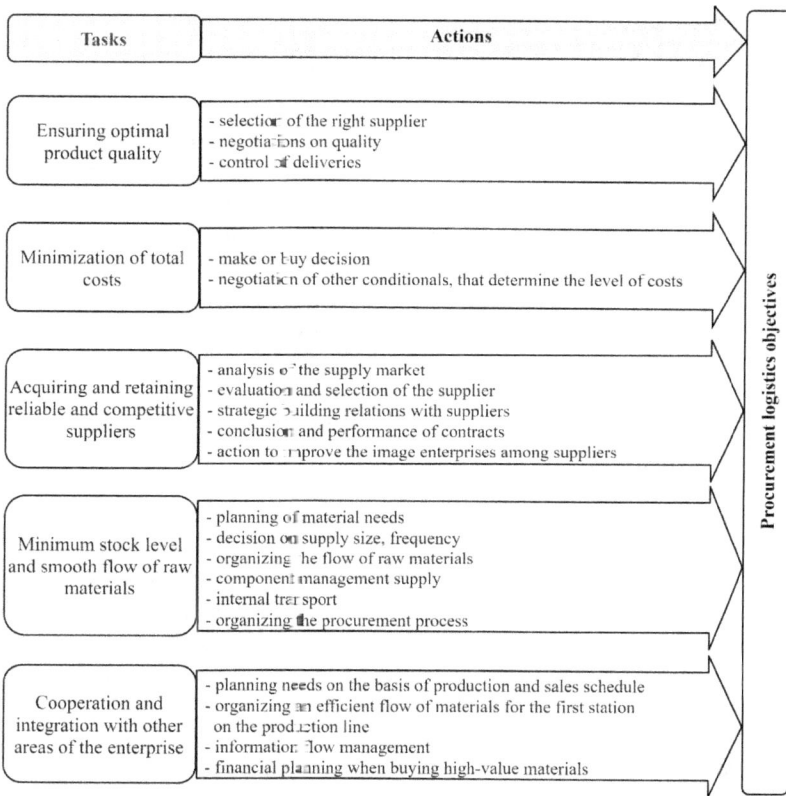

Figure 3.1 Procurement logistics objectives divided into tasks and activities Source: Authors' own study on the basis of Abt (1998).

Materials management, procurement, and procurement logistics are key issues, knowledge of which in both theoretical and practical contexts seems to be a *sine qua non* for a proper understanding of the nature of the logistics audit of procurement; especially since the concept itself in this form is quite rarely used and therefore little known, which is also confirmed in the literature devoted to audit issues, including internal or industry audit. Therefore, when attempting to define the logistics audit of procurement, we can conclude that it is a tool for regular review of logistics activities in the area of procurement, whose task is to assess the compliance of the state of implementation of processes related to the planning of materials needs, selection of suppliers, and organization of supply supplies with the procedures, regulations, and instructions in force in the enterprise. The final product of a logistics audit of procurement should be suggestions and recommendations that will serve to further improve the processes, structures, and procedures in the procurement subsystem of the organization's logistics system. The development of such a forward-looking approach is also intended to reduce and eliminate all the risks that occur in this subsystem, and which may be associated with late delivery, non-compliance of delivery with the order, incorrect planning (also forecasting) of materials needs, volatility of market prices of materials and exchange rates, internal defects of materials revealed in the course of production, errors or deficiencies in the production documentation regarding offers, orders, commercial contracts, certificates, and a decrease in supply (i.e., an increase in costs) of materials used in the production process.

The starting point in the implementation of a logistics audit of procurement should be a thorough verification of the method of planning material requirements in an enterprise (material requirements planning (MRP)). In practice, this approach allows the auditor, on the one hand, to reliably assess the rationalization of materials supply-planning in the enterprise, and on the other hand, to recognize the degree of optimization of the procurement process in the organization's logistics system. For this purpose, it is necessary to estimate the market primary demand (independent needs) and secondary (dependent needs),[3] which will become the basis for the auditor to holistically evaluate the correctness of planning material needs in the enterprise. In addition to planning material needs, the logistics audit of procurement will focus its attention on:

- order processing processes (including complaints and returns),
- verification of the conformity of deliveries with orders,
- methods of assessment, verification, and relations with suppliers,
- degree of speed, response, and flexibility of the operation of the entire supply subsystem,
- bottlenecks in supply logistics processes,
- costs of handling orders,
- free flow of information and financial and material resources in procurement processes.

Among the areas of interest in the logistics audit of procurement presented above, special attention should be paid to the issue related to the assessment, verification, and – ultimately – selection of suppliers. The point is that the right choice of suppliers is one of the most important issues in the field of supply logistics. Therefore, the activities of the logistics audit of procurement in the sphere of supplier selection should focus primarily on (Jezierski, 2007b):

- assessment of the choice of suppliers – it is necessary to take into account which supplier best meets the requirements presented to the customer, what distance separates the supplier from the supply warehouse, what the rhythmicity and timeliness of deliveries is, what the quantitative and qualitative possibilities of deliveries in emergency situations (i.e., crisis or emergency) are,
- analysis of the form of cooperation with suppliers – the type and form of the concluded contract, provisions on the possibility and conditions of negotiating prices, rules on contractual penalties, the duration of the cooperation agreement, and the provisions on its prolongation may be verified,
- examination of elements of the supply subsystem related to the quality of supply – identifying, verifying, and improving mechanisms (persons, tools, and footnotes) supervising the quality of supply deliveries,
- review whether the supplier can be considered a so-called qualified supplier – examining the list of qualified suppliers in terms of their competence and ability to meet the criteria set for them by the recipient.[4]

In practice, the logistics audit of procurement in the sphere of suppliers should be carried out more often in relation to strategic suppliers, since it is on their supplies that the possibility of continuing the core business of the enterprise depends.

Finally, it should be emphasized that procurement logistics should be carried out especially in production enterprises, where a significant part of the costs of the production process are those resulting from procurement. In this type of organization, the purchase price of raw materials, materials, or parts strongly determines the costs of finished products, which, in the final stage, has an impact on the margin achieved from the sale of the organization's goods.

3.2. Logistics audit of production

Discussing the issues related to the logistics audit of production requires – in the first place – familiarization with the basic concepts in the field of production theory, which will determine the shape, form, and structure of this type of audit. Therefore, the terms discussed at the beginning of this chapter will refer primarily to what the product, production (production process), and production management are. So, when it comes to the definition of the word "product," it should be emphasized that often in economics it is focused strictly on the consumer, i.e., the user of a specific product or service, who always perceives the product (or service) through the prism of broadly understood applications. Meanwhile – especially in the context of participants in the production process – "product" is a term interpreted differently by the production manager, the financial manager, or the personnel manager. In the case of the former, the product will be everything that "builds" the product, i.e., production area (hall), tools, machines, processes, operations, etc. Thus, the optimal, and therefore the most beneficial in given conditions, use of the possessed set of goods will be conducive to the creation of final products that will be characterized by a high level of market competitiveness. For people dealing with enterprise finances, a product is primarily a set of different costs that shape the final price of the product and – what is important – determine its break-even point.[5] The product is perceived differently by people who deal with human resources management in the organization on a daily basis. For them, the product is the skills and qualifications of employees that are necessary to produce a specific type of product or service. To sum up, it can therefore be assumed – in a broad sense – that a product is a thing with material or immaterial characteristics, which serves to satisfy the specific needs of specific people. In practice, all products are manufactured in the production process. So far, in management science, the word "production" has received rich interpretation and many definitions. One of the most concise is that production is the activity of producing some goods and/or services. However, the production of goods, as Duda (1997) rightly points out, also requires adequate materials, a human labor force, and the necessary technical skills. In other words, production is a process – taking place in a certain time and space – that transforms available resources (material and intangible) into finished products, thus satisfying the needs of individuals, households, societies, and nations. The issue of the production process satisfying the specific needs of others was also raised in the definition presented by Hicks, in which production is any activity planned to meet the needs of others through exchange (Aliyu, 2019). Bearing in mind the definitions of production proposed by Hicks and the authors of this study, there arises the fundamental question whether the production of goods – within the framework of economics – that does not take into account the context relating to the necessity of satisfying, by these goods, the specific needs of individuals, can be considered production in the strict sense. The answer appears to be no. In economics we consider as production only those activities related to the provision of goods and services to the market that serve to meet the specific needs of consumers. This means that in economics the terms production and manufacturing should not be used interchangeably, because they are not equivalent terms. In practice, the production process can be carried out in three basic ways (Nassab et al., 2013):

- production by disintegration, which consists of separating the content of a given substance or agent from the main product. An example are the modern technologies that use a porous material called polystyrene acrylate and sunlight to separate salt from seawater. As a result of using this technique, we obtain products in the form of sea salt and drinking water,

- production by integration, which in practice is the opposite of production by disintegration and consists in combining (merging) various components into one whole. As a result, we get the product we want that satisfies our needs. An example is a building material in the form of dry concrete, which is formed by mixing cement, aggregate, additives, and a small amount of water,
- production by services, which boils down to the "refinement" of the product as a result of the activities (services) to which it is subjected. An example is the production of a diamond, which is made by grinding a diamond (precious stone) according to a diamond cut (a service performed by a jeweler).

Considering the above, we see that production is in fact a transformative activity that concerns not only goods but also services. As a result, the input data is transformed into output data, which can change in terms of form, shape, structure, volume, weight, place, or time. The end result of this process, however, is a definite good that has value, both utilitarian and economic.

The last concept, apart from product and production, which needs clarification in the context of a logistics audit of production, is production management. In a narrow sense, production management should be understood as planning, organizing, directing, and controlling processes related to the production activity of the enterprise, which are aimed at transforming – in an optimal way – raw materials into final products. However, in broad terms, production management can be defined as a holistic system of management that transforms input resources into products and services desired by consumers. Although the definitions presented above do not express it directly, it should be emphasized that the responsibility for the production process lies both with the management of the organization and with the employees who are to jointly implement specific goals according to the adopted rules, schedules, and specifications. The result of their collective work, done correctly, may be the creation of an effective production management system, which we will be able to talk about only if the goods delivered to the recipient meet quality and quantity expectations, while maintaining optimization in the implementation of production processes.

Moving directly to the issue of logistics audit of production, it should be noted at the outset that not only in management literature but also in professional and trade journals, the subject of logistics audit of production is

– to date – little discussed. This situation is caused by several factors. First of all, the logistics audit of production is a novelty on the market of audit services both in Poland and abroad. Secondly, industry audits (to which logistics audit belongs) are positions that are still poorly established in both theory and practice. Thirdly, there is a noticeable lack of specialists who could skillfully combine several years of experience in the field of logistics with their competences in the field of internal audit. And fourthly, the last gap is in the formation of professional groups or associations, which would be bodies bringing together specialists, advisors, managers, and scientists in the field of logistics and audit, whose task would focus primarily on building and developing the framework of the logistics audit methodology. Therefore, taking into account the above-mentioned limitations, which slow down the dynamics of knowledge growth in the field of the logistics audit of production, it is important to define its essence. In broad terms, a logistics audit of production is an evaluation of production logistics, which takes into account the identification of processes requiring improvement and places where unjustified production costs arise. Thus, through the logistics audit of production, one of the key principles regarding the management of the organization is implemented, related to the optimization of the costs of doing business. In a narrow sense, we will define the logistics audit of production as advisory and management activities aimed at all aspects related to the improvement of the production process, in areas related to production planning, procurement, storage, marking, reporting, and the flow of raw materials inside the production hall. Therefore, we can conclude that, in practice, a logistics audit of production is a diagnosis of the current state of production, which is the result of partial assessments, in the form of:

- an organization of work in the area of production,
- a process of planning, organizing, and controlling production,
- a flow of raw materials, semi-finished products, semi-finished products,
- a method of algorithmizing and parameterizing production,
- a system of comprehensive management of the organization through quality (total quality management (TQM)),[6]
- internal logistics (internal transport),[7]
- forces of purchasing and warehouse economies affecting the production process,
- production losses,
- a system of information flow and communication in the production process.

The main goal of the logistics audit of production is to add value and increase the degree of functionalization of the production logistics of a given enterprise, through factual and conceptual support of the decision-making process in the area of the logistics system of the organization. However, in order to achieve the basic goal, auxiliary purposes are to be used, which include:

- a thorough assessment of enterprise production logistics on the basis of the adopted criteria,
- improving operational activities,
- optimization of the use of the enterprise's production resources,
- reduction or elimination of groups of disturbances occurring in logistics processes related to procurement, production, distribution, transport, and storage,
- setting priorities for the proper implementation of the enterprise's production logistics.

The above-mentioned objectives of the logistics audit of production are implemented with the help of various methods,[8] techniques, and research tools, including document research, analysis of existing data (data mining,[9] business intelligence[10]), quantitative analyses, observations, tests, interviews, case studies, physical measurements, key performance indicators,[11] etc. Due to the fact that the logistics audit of production is a voluntary service, and therefore not resulting from the provisions of the law, it can be used by every enterprise, production- and distribution-oriented, and any others. Therefore, neither the specificity of the enterprise (its size or structure), nor the scope of its activity, nor the sector or industry in which it operates are relevant here. In other words, the recipients of the services in the form of the logistics audit of production can be all organizations whose representatives want to check and identify imperfections occurring in the production logistics system subordinate to them. The key factors determining the choice of a logistics audit of production as a tool to optimize activities in this area include:

- the need to rationalize production costs,
- the need to identify and eliminate sources affecting the inefficiency of the entire production area,
- the desire to increase labor productivity,
- the intention to improve the planning and organization of production,
- the need to reorganize and functionalize the layout of the production hall,
- the need to ensure an optimal level of stocks for critical products,
- the need to report, control, and monitor the production process,
- the desire to eliminate many disturbances occurring in the production process,

- the intention to reduce the number of complaints,
- the need to ensure traceability of serial numbers or production batches,
- the need to improve logistics parameters,
- the desire to increase the motivation and knowledge of employees about the implemented improvements.

Thus, the benefits that an organization can derive from including a logistics audit in the process of improving the efficiency of operational components of the logistics system are as significant and real as they are numerous and diverse. First, the organization's managers can count on the correctness of diagnoses made in problem areas that have been the subject of audit research. Second, taking into account the most favorable solutions in given conditions, managers can count on the fact that the decisions taken will save both time and financial resources. Third, thanks to the audit, the organization can be sure that the solutions used are a derivative of the best patterns and techniques that have been developed in this field so far. Fourth, the possibility of making incorrect decisions to protect the organization against losses related to the cost of risk are minimized. And fifth, an organization can focus on what it does best and what it specializes in.

To sum up, it should be emphasized that the logistics audit of production, when regularly conducted, builds large data sets on the logistics system of the organization, which, when properly transformed, will provide information and knowledge about the possibilities of improving its efficiency (Voortman, 2004).

3.3. The logistics audit of the warehouse

The subject of this chapter is the logistics audit of the warehouse. The discussion of this issue will be preceded by the presentation of the basic conceptual apparatus, which, on the basis of theory, is to provide a better understanding of the described category. The basic concepts permanently tied to the logistics audit of the warehouse include warehouse, warehousing, and warehouse management. On the basis of logistics, a warehouse can be concisely defined as a place of storage (keeping) of goods. However, if we wanted to refer to more extensive definitions of this concept, it is worth noting the one developed by Gołembska (2007a), in which a warehouse is a unit dealing with the storage of material products that are temporarily excluded from use, having a space separated for this purpose, as well as technical means intended for the transport of stocks and their handling. Nevertheless, the term is described by Bartholdi and Hackman (2006), for whom it is a facility in the supply chain for the consolidation of products in order to reduce transport costs and achieve economies of scale in production or purchasing. Although each of the definitions presented above emphasizes the various features of a warehouse, their common denominator is that a warehouse is an object (building) that has a specific function related to the storage of goods (materials). And although an important function, it is not the only one that warehouses perform in many organizations. A conceptual category closely coupled with warehouses is warehousing. In theory, it has received many interpretations and definitional approaches. This is a result of the different perspectives from which researchers approach this issue. Nevertheless, in a broad sense, as proposed by Razik et al. (2017), warehousing is defined as a process that groups all the activities that permit a warehouse to be designed, defines the means and tools necessary for its functioning, identifies warehouse operations, and effectively manages them. Both in theory and practice, the process related to warehousing[12] consists of four basic phases:[13] the receipt phase, the storage phase, the picking phase, and the shipment of material goods. All of them must be properly planned, organized, and controlled. However, the storage and picking phases deserve special attention, especially by managers, as they are the most complex and labor-intensive among all phases. In addition, they largely determine the level of warehouse performance. As the course of the storage process can be multidimensional and multithreaded at the same time, it is graphically presented in Figure 3.2. The last element that needs to be explained, in the context of considering the logistics audit of a warehouse, is the concept of warehouse management. The function it performs in the management of the efficient enterprise is important because it is the warehouse, as part of the logistics infrastructure, that implies the flow of resources, materials, and finished products between suppliers and final recipients. In synthetic terms, warehouse management is an activity consisting of managing the technical, organizational, and economic aspects of the warehouse's operation in the field of receiving, storing, picking, and issuing goods, while maintaining constant control over the processes and functions carried out. Thus, warehouse management focuses on the control and optimization of complex warehouse and distribution processes and is interdependent both on the tasks assigned to it and on the market in which the warehouses operate (DeKoster & Smidts, 2013). However, due to the dynamic development of the digital economy, effective warehouse management cannot be currently implemented without the participation of tools whose construction is based on artificial intelligence technology or machine-learning algorithms.

Having basic knowledge in the field of business logistics and warehousing, we can proceed to discuss the concept of the logistics audit of the warehouse. From a definitional point of view, a logistics audit of the warehouse – in synthetic terms – is an assessment of the state of warehouse logistics of an enterprise in the area of cargo planning and management

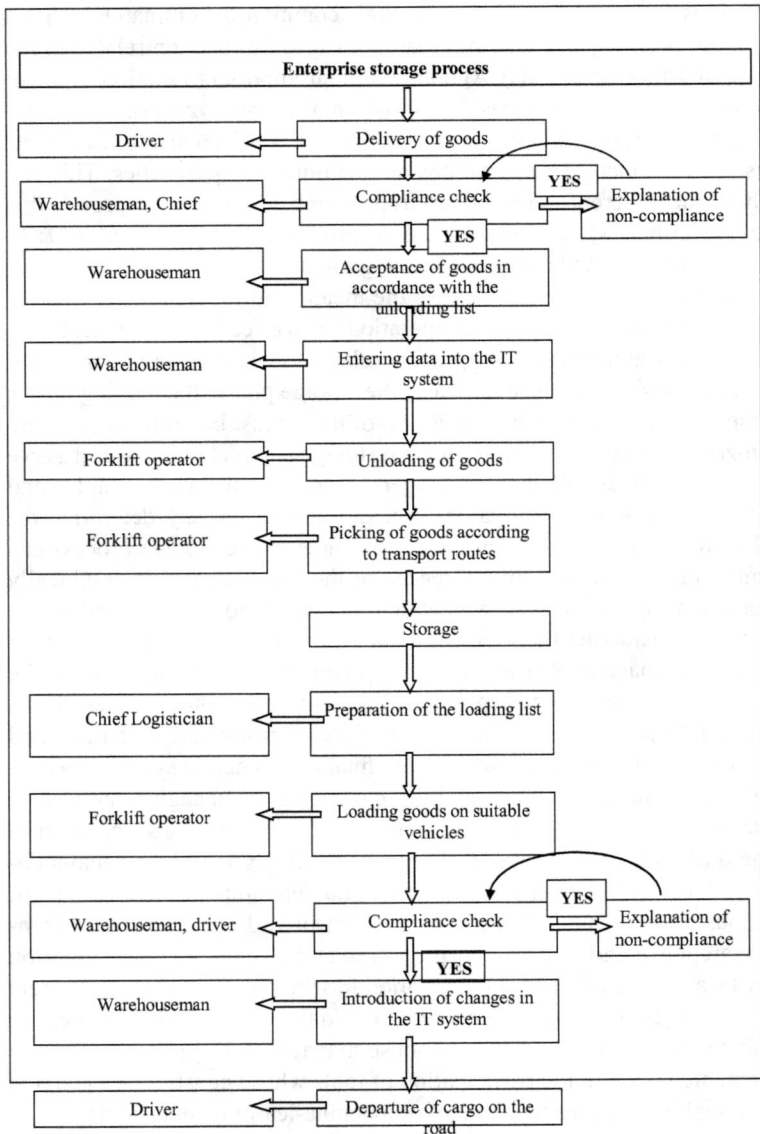

Figure 3.2 Storage process in the organization – graphical example Source: Rut and Miłasiewicz, 2016, p. 27.

and their handling in the field of receiving, storing, and shipping. Its scope covers all aspects of the enterprise's operation related to storage, including the improvement of processes and functions that are carried out in the warehouse and its close surroundings. Thanks to the evaluation – in terms of quality or complexity – of the stream of warehouse activities processing input elements into output elements, the productivity and efficiency of warehouse logistics is improved. As a consequence, activities in the entire transport and warehouse chain, which is the basis for the functioning of the supply chain in the organization, are also improved.

The logistics audit of the warehouse, like the logistics audit of production or distribution, is discretionary. This means that the management has full freedom in its planning and organization, in relation to both the organizational unit located inside the organization and to an external institution. In a narrow sense, we will understand the logistics audit of the warehouse as a thorough analysis of the elements (and the links between them) included in the storage subsystem of the enterprise's logistics system, the purpose of which is to get to know it, examine it, draw conclusions, and make the correct diagnosis in the way it operates. At the same time, this type of approach to the definition of a logistics audit of the warehouse cannot fail to take into account the impact that external factors have on warehouse processes, even in the legal and administrative dimension of the environment of each organization. The common denominator for the presented definitions is primarily the desire of the logistics audit to identify and then improve problem areas that affect the work of the warehouse, which then affects the overall logistics potential[14] of the organization. In general, a logistics audit of the warehouse has a number of goals to achieve, which can be divided into general and partial (specific). The general purposes of the logistics audit of the warehouse include:

- identification of problem areas, limitations, deviations, and inefficiencies in the sphere of warehouse management of the organization,
- optimization of warehouse logistics costs,
- increasing the degree of efficiency of activities carried out in the area of storage and warehouse management,
- reducing or eliminating errors and/or aberrations occurring in warehouse operations,
- increasing the efficiency of inventory management,
- optimization of warehouse space,
- identification and elimination of activities that do not add value to the storage subsystem of the organization's logistics system.

However, among the partial objectives of the logistics audit of the warehouse, we can distinguish:

- increasing the efficiency of processes carried out in the storage subsystem of the organization's logistics system,
- improvement of the strategy and directions of development of warehouse logistics,
- optimization of operating costs in the areas of storage, maintenance of warehouses, and utilities,
- increasing the use of people's potential and warehouse and handling infrastructure,
- elimination of bottlenecks in warehouse processes,
- increasing the productivity of the warehouse by increasing the degree of its automation,
- identification and elimination of activities that do not add value.

The implementation of selected goals that the logistics audit of the warehouse in the logistics system of the organization has to meet gives rise, in practice, to important knowledge about both the efficiency of its operation and the degree of use of its logistics potential, especially in the area of warehouse management. As a result, the management team have objective information about the state of the enterprise's logistics and can use it to correctly formulate strategies and directions for the development of warehouse logistics or to redefine them. The question arises about the additional benefits that the organization can additionally derive from the implementation of a logistics audit of the warehouse. In synthetic terms, they may concern:

- the ability to make the right decisions that save time, money, and resources of the enterprise,
- the reduction of risks, including human error risk, financial risk, operational risk, market risk, business risk, or even bankruptcy risk,
- reducing operating costs and opportunity costs,
- better use of the tangible and intangible resources of the enterprise,
- the possibility of adopting solutions that have been recognized as "best practice" in the global economy,
- the possibility of focusing on important activities and abandoning non-important ones (prioritization of tasks),
- strengthening and improving the internal control system,
- improving efforts to achieve sustainable warehouse management.

At the end of this chapter devoted to the issue of warehouse logistics audit, it should be added that this type of industry audit may cover a fragment, a part, or an area of warehouse logistics, as well as the entire spectrum of issues related to it. Thus, the research subject of logistics audit of the warehouse is the broadly understood "warehouse reality," which consists of warehouse infrastructure, handling infrastructure, warehouse IT systems, warehouse documentation, flow of materials, and information and financial resources in warehouse management. In addition, it also covers the processes, relationships, dependencies, or relationships that occur between the elements of the storage subsystem in the enterprise's logistics system. All the above-mentioned elements can be tested from the point of view of logistical audit in various aspects and using various research methods, including observational, statistical, comparative, diagnostic, heuristic,[15] documentary, or experimental research. In other words, this means that in practice, the logistics audit in warehousing is not limited, either in terms of the scope itself, the methods adopted to scientifically understand the problems of warehouse logistics, or the size of the organization that may be subject to it.

3.4. Logistics audit of distribution

Nowadays, it is impossible to imagine the functioning of an enterprise without a supply chain, which is considered one of the most extensive processes in the science of organization and management. Its holistic understanding, taking into account the product life cycle, sales service, or disposal, is often referred to as the value chain (or Porter's value chain).[16] The point is that in the process of producing goods, all the elements present in it determine the final value that the organization provides to the environment, both task-oriented and general. An inseparable part of the supply chain – in addition to supply and production – is distribution, which is considered a key element of the economic process. Due to its place in the enterprise's logistics activities, it plays a leading role in achieving its economic and marketing objectives. In practice, this is confirmed by the increase in enterprise profitability indicators,[17] which are conducive not only to its stabilization and development but above all to higher profits. This means that a well-thought-out distribution model integrated with the other subsystems of the enterprise's logistics system can become an element of fundamental importance in the winning strategy of each organization. The very concept of distribution based on management science[18] is defined as a process – i.e., a sequence of successive causally related changes – of the movement of goods between the producer and the consumer. As Domschke and Schild (1994) point out, the goods produced are prepared in a coordinated manner according to their type and size and taking into account space and time, so that delivery deadlines can be met or the volume of demand on the market can be met.

In broad terms, we can therefore conclude that distribution describes all the logistics related to the delivery of the enterprise's products and services to the recipient, taking into account their final place, delivery time, and costs. However, the proper course of this process will be the result of the degree of integration of the physical flow of goods, information, and financial resources with the functions carried out within the organization in the areas of planning, organization, and control. Nowadays, distribution, as one of the most important links in the logistics chain, is the fastest-growing sphere of logistics activity in economies, especially in developing countries. What's more, at the level of enterprises, it is often set as a benchmark in defining their market successes or failures.[19] The main goal of distribution is primarily to guarantee the fastest possible course of the process while maintaining the most favorable level of quality of consumer service in given conditions. Simply put, in other words it is about managing the supply chain in such a way that the flow of materials, information, and financial resources between the supplier and the end user will make it as fast as possible. However, in addition to the main goal, distribution also has to achieve a number of other, no less important, so-called side goals, which will include (Śliżewska & Zadrożna, 2014):

- optimization of order handling,
- optimization of the transport process,
- minimizing the time of distribution processes in such a way that the product reaches the final recipient as soon as possible,
- improving the level of consumer service,
- minimization of distribution costs,
- selection of an appropriate distribution channel.

In practice, the implementation of even a few of the selected goals referred to here can be a real challenge for the enterprise. Activities that on the one hand assume, for example, constant improvement of the level of quality of services provided among customers, and on the other hand, regular reduction of costs, are problematic in their implementation. Therefore, achieving goals in the area of distribution requires the management of the enterprise to make many decisions and perform a number of tasks; if these are not mutually exclusive, the desire to implement them in combination requires a lot of commitment and knowledge. All this must be supplemented and supported by organizational and coordination activities, because any disturbances in this respect may ultimately affect the success or failure of the organization in its pursuit of the strategic goal.[20]

The concepts inextricably linked to the distribution process, as evidenced by logistics itself, are distribution logistics and distribution channels. Distribution logistics is an activity that focuses on the implementation of activities in the sales network, from production planning to customer after-sales service. Thus, the activities carried out as part of distribution logistics cover a wide range of issues, starting from the study of market needs and the assessment of demand for the offered products, through production and sales, ending with customer service, including the after-sales service (Nowakowska, 2019). In an enterprise, distribution logistics can appear both as an element of marketing or as a normal distribution activity. In the first of these cases, distribution consists mainly in managing the activities of suppliers, production processes, optimizing the flow of products from suppliers to potential buyers to meet their requirements, while in the second, in the physical flow of products from the starting point to the destination, at the lowest possible costs and using specific distribution channels (Śliżewska & Zadrożna, 2014). Nowadays, the keen interest in distribution logistics among the managers of enterprises results from the need to gradually reduce relatively high distribution costs, especially in relation to the constantly growing competition and decreasing profitability of enterprises. In addition, alternative solutions are constantly being sought to achieve new competitive advantages of the enterprise on the market, not only in the areas of customer service standards but also – and perhaps above all – of the product. The second of the previously mentioned concepts is the distribution channel in which all distribution operations and activities are performed. The distribution channel is defined in management literature, e.g., by Oklander (2005) and Larina (2005), as a chain arranged linearly by operations, which helps the physical flow of the product from one intermediary to another, up to the end user. In other words, we can say that the distribution channel is in practice a collection of all entities through which (deliberately) there is a real flow of goods, services, information, and financial resources. At this point, it should be added that planning, and then building, a distribution channel is in practice a difficult task. Andjelkovic and Radosavljevic (2020) argue that it often poses many problems and raises the need to make important – from the point of view of the enterprise – decisions and choices regarding the type of channel (direct, indirect), number of entities involved, coverage (long, short), width (narrow or wide), and type of intermediaries (wholesaler, retailer, agent). In the context of this, Figure 3.3 shows – in simple terms – the existing possibilities for designing distribution channels, taking into account those elements referred to.

At this point it should be emphasized that the choices and the activities that the managerial staff undertakes and implements in the area of distribution channels and distribution logistics affect the holistic assessment of the degree of effectiveness of the distribution system[21] of an enterprise. As a result, the efficiency of distribution (see Figure 3.4) indicates the level of its ability to achieve the set goals, generate higher turnover from the sale of products and services, and gain a privileged position on the market in relation to other entities operating on it.

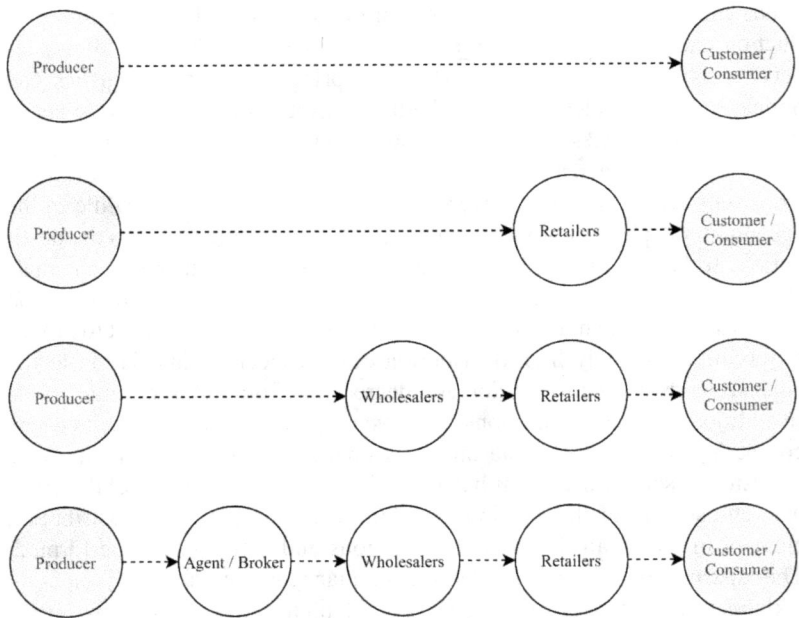

Figure 3.3 Typology of distribution channels – a comparative approach Source: Authors' own study based on Kotler (2010, p. 420).

The conceptual framework in the field of distribution logistics presented above provides a good basis for an attempt to define the logistics audit of distribution as one of the types of logistics audit. We can therefore assume that the logistics audit of distribution is – in broad terms – a systemic and expert look at the distribution subsystem in the enterprise's logistics system, in order to determine whether it meets the expectations and requirements set for it by the organization's stakeholders. However, in a narrow sense, it is an independent study consisting of acquiring (new) knowledge in the areas of storage, transport, inventory management, order fulfillment, and marketing, the aim of which is to assess the actual state of the distribution subsystem, including its potential, as well as to recommend improvement activities. In practice, the logistics audit of distribution will therefore focus on a systematic review of the entire distribution activity of the organization, in terms of the effectiveness of using its tangible and intangible resources, as well as the correctness of the functioning of processes. In addition, it will also indirectly assess the distribution potential of the organization in the logistics of the entire enterprise (see Figure 3.5).

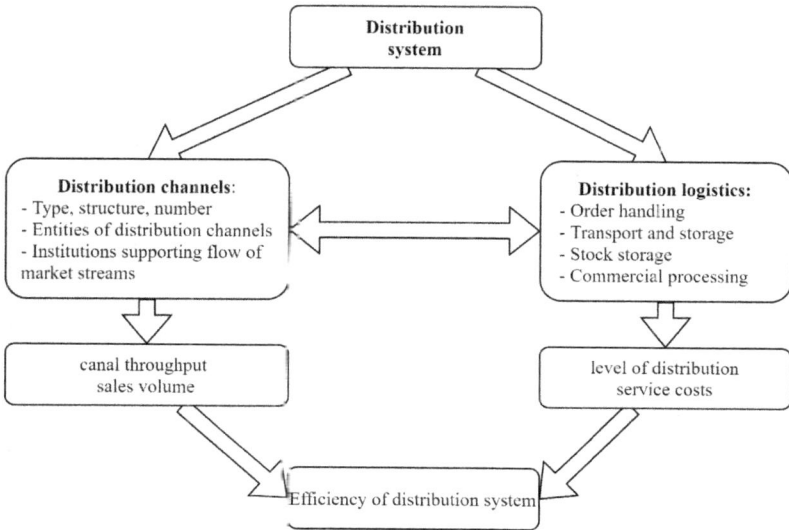

Figure 3.4 Efficient distribution system model Source: Authors' own study based on Altkorn (2004, p. 196).

Its main objectives, as an industry audit in the field of logistics, primarily include:

- assistance in making better decisions regarding the development of the enterprise's distribution system,
- assessment of whether the resources and potential of the distribution subsystem in the enterprise's logistics system are in line with the current requirements and capabilities both in terms of the whole and the components,
- identification of the strengths and weaknesses of distribution activities and systems supporting them,
- minimizing risks and accidents related to the functioning of distribution logistics,
- increasing customer satisfaction with internal and external customers from improving the quality of network operation and distribution channels,
- development of recommendations to implement the improvements proposed as a result of the logistics audit of distribution.

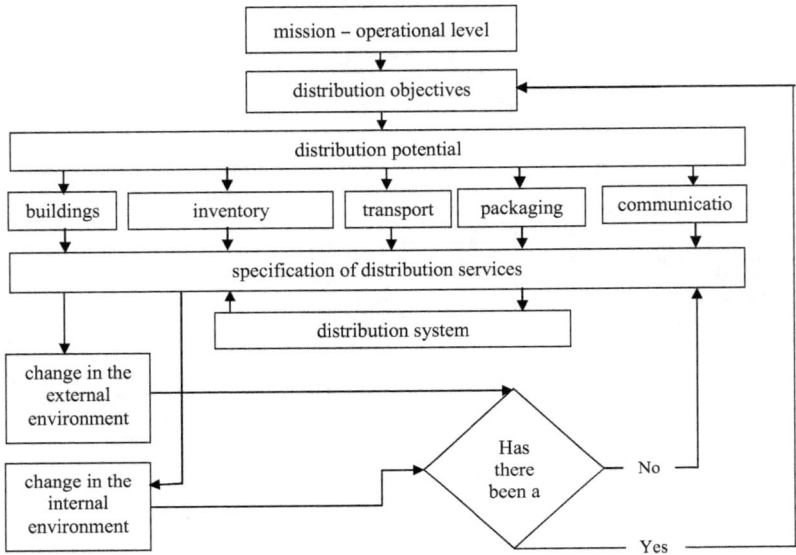

Figure 3.5 Distribution potential of the organization – reference conditions Source: based on Emerald Publishing Limited (1988, pp. 78–82).

Since the logistics audit of distribution is a complex issue, there are a large number of areas that can be subject to it in the enterprise logistics system. Nevertheless, most often, the logistics audit of distribution is subject to:

- technical and organizational distribution of the logistics network,
- structure, layout, type of flowing streams, and entities of distribution channels,
- vertical and horizontal integration of distribution channels,[22]
- processes including such activities as managing relations between entities involved in the delivery of products to end users, the flow and movement of goods, organizing and supervising the flow of information and financial resources, building sales channels, etc.,
- route of flow of materials, information, financial resources, and documents,
- ways, methods, and techniques for designing and organizing distribution,
- cost-creating areas of distribution logistics (see Table 3.1 and Figure 3.6),
- optimization of distribution transport.

Table 3.1 Logistics audit of distribution – cost-creating areas

Internal environment	Product costs	Seasonality
		Costs of distribution of new products
	Distribution model	Stocks
		Storage
		Use of the fleet
		Level of customer service
		Shopping
	Type of object	Procurement costs
		Warehouse costs
		Transport costs
		Inventory costs
		Overheads
External environment	Marketing factors	Transport costs
		Warehouse costs
		Inventory maintenance costs
	Competition	Location of competitors
		Strength of competitors
	Distribution channels	Channel structure
		Costs of distribution channels
	Government regulations	Manufacturers
		Transport
		Storage
		Packaging

Source: Authors' own study based on Lancioni, 1991, pp. 13–14.

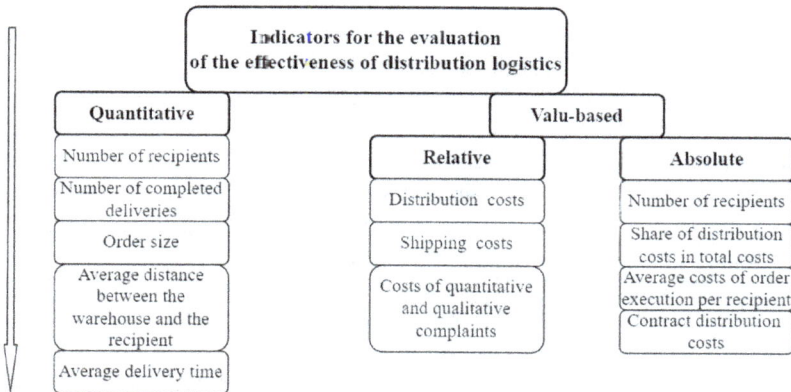

Figure 3.6 Assessment of distribution logistics Source: Authors' own study based on Nowicka-Skowron (2000, p. 29).

In the conclusion of this chapter on the issue of logistical audit of distri-bution, a few general remarks should be made. First, the logistics audit of distribution, as a type of logistics audit, although not yet recognized, makes an important contribution to the development of industry audits, as a modern tool supporting the basic functions carried out in the area of organization management. Second, it provides managers with valuable information on the appropriateness and effectiveness of the existing distribution subsystem in the enterprise's logistics system and the quality of its operation. Third, the distribution logistics audit provides an opportunity to identify those areas within the enterprise's distribution logistics that have the greatest capabilities and potential for "self-development." Fourth, it is a tool for critically assess-ing the activities of those responsible for supervising the enterprise's distribu-tion logistics. And fifth, such audits promote pro-developmental changes in the area of broadly understood business distribution logistics and act as a cat-alyst for development processes in the logistics systems of the organization.

3.5. Logistics audit of the supply chain

Today, due to the global nature of most enterprises, supply chains are becoming longer and therefore more complex. As a consequence, this leads to an arithmetic increase in the risk of disruption, which in the context of the supply chain is perceived as something that requires special supervi-sion and control by the management of an organization. In a somewhat natural way, such a situation gives rise to notable interest in this process, also for the audit itself, which aspires to be a tool for improving enterprise activities. However, the discussion in this section, the content of which is a logistics audit of the supply chain, requires first of all the definition of the concept of supply chain, which, incidentally, in logistics, is the object of many interpretative and contextual approaches. One of them, by Pienaar (2009), defines the supply chain as a synthetic description of the integra-tion of a process that engages the resources of the organization in order to transform raw materials into final products and deliver them to the final recipient. Another definition, proposed by Chow and Heaver (1999), pre-sents the entities (groups) that make up the supply chain: manufacturers, suppliers, distributors, retailers or wholesalers, which are involved in sup-plying customers with goods purchased by them. In practice, we can there-fore conclude that the supply chain is essentially a coordinated process in which goods physically flow from their place of origin to their destina-tion, accompanied in parallel by the flow of funds, intangible resources, and information (see Figure 3.7).

Knowledge of the term supply chain now entitles us to try to define the essence of the issue, which in this chapter is the logistics audit of the supply

Relationship management

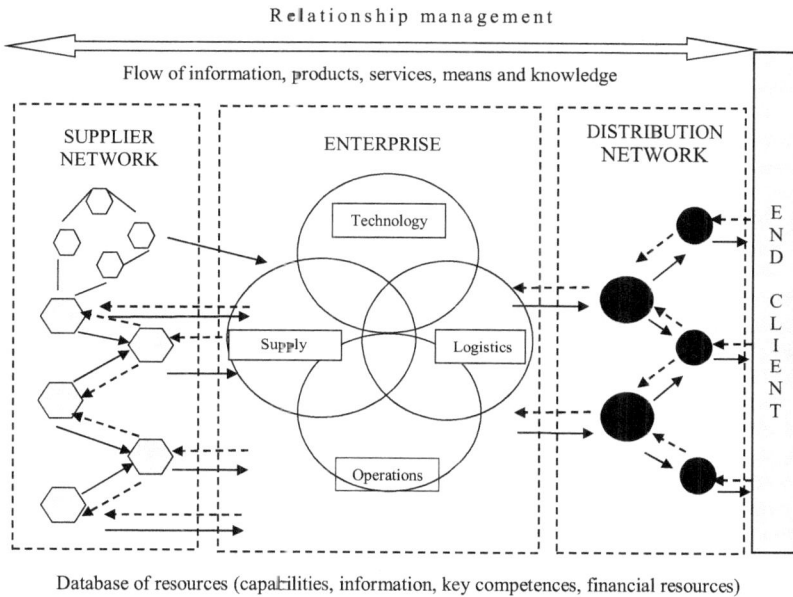

Figure 3.7 Integrated supply chain Source: based on Handfield and Nicols, 2002, p. 39.

chain. Thus, through a logistics audit of the supply chain, we understand a process aimed at improving the physical flow of goods, financial resources, intangible resources, and information in the supply chain, in order to increase its efficiency within a given organization. Improving the supply chain in the area of logistics audit consists both in the use of best practices and practices that are used in other industries and sectors and in the use of quantitative and qualitative research methods and techniques. Their final results are the basic material for developing new concepts, ideas, and solutions in modernizing the productivity of supply chains. A logistics audit of the supply chain is therefore a key tool with which management can identify and then solve the root causes of problems that occur in supply-chain logistics. Their scale, complexity, and multifaceted nature can take on different characters and be present at different levels of the organization, including at the strategic, operational, or tactical levels. What's more, gaps and deviations may also manifest themselves in the further internal environment of the enterprise, in relation to its suppliers, customers, strategic partners, co-operators, etc. A logistics audit of the supply chain is therefore a comprehensive audit that covers a wide spectrum of events that occur not only in the endogenous layer of the supply chain but also between the entities that create it. As a result, its implementation contributes not only to the synthetic improvement of supply-chain logistics, but also to the reduction of operating costs or the improvement of market competitiveness. On the other hand, the basic objectives of a logistics audit of the supply chain should be considered tasks aimed at:

- independent assessment of logistics activities carried out within the supply chain of a given organization,
- identification of weak (but also strong) points that characterize supply-chain logistics,
- improvement of logistics processes taking place in the area of the supply chain,
- identification of areas in the supply chain that need improvement.

Using existing supply-chain audit concepts and methodologies, a logistics audit of the supply chain can take many forms, including:[23]

- deep logistics audit of the supply chain – an audit that aims to familiarize itself precisely and thoroughly with the logistics processes taking place in the supply chain of an enterprise, taking into account its organizational structure, adopted business model, purchasing and supply structures, organizational environment, and competences and qualifications,
- comprehensive logistics audit of the supply chain – an audit that covers all logistics processes taking place in the subsystems of the logistics system related (directly or indirectly) to the supply chain,
- simple logistics audit of the supply chain – an audit that may concern a selected logistics process (its part or a single task) in the supply chain,
- quick logistics audit of the supply chain – an audit carried out in a short period of time, which is characterized by a narrow form, dedicated mainly to senior management, consisting in conducting simple research aimed at quickly identifying the problem and inhibiting activities that may directly affect the profit and loss account of an entity. These types of audits, however, require quick access to high-quality data.

The forms of the logistics audit of the supply chain presented above can, in practice, be carried out in various enterprises, including technological, production, trade, retail, export, import, or service. Nevertheless, in order for a logistics audit of the supply chain to be considered – apart from its form – as effective, in practice it must meet several basic conditions. First, it requires securing adequate human resources necessary to prepare an audit plan, carry out audit activities related to data collection and analysis, monitor the audit process, or develop results and proposals for improvements. Second, every audit – not only the one concerning the logistics audit of the supply chain – requires high-level specialist knowledge, which is why it should involve in its activities those people who have qualifications adequate to the subject of the tasks performed and the challenges awaiting them. Third – although it is not conclusive – the effectiveness of the audit is often determined through the prism of good knowledge of the organization, the environment in which it operates, its stakeholders, local customs, and accepted norms of behavior or values professed in an environment. Fourth, the aim should be to ensure that the audit is carried out primarily in situ rather than remotely, especially where there are differences of a linguistic, national, cultural, and even religious or political nature. Fifth, the measurement tools used in the audit should reflect the content, scale, and complexity of the issues examined. And sixth, an effective audit cannot do without providing adequate access to large amounts of high-quality data.

Taking into account the above, but also the contemporary conditions in which supply chains operate, it should be concluded that the implementation of a logistics audit in this area may be a difficult task, requiring also – and perhaps above all – knowledge of the concept of supply chain management. The point is that in many organizations there are different models of the supply chain, which are harmonized with the specifics of their activities. This gives rise to further challenges in the implementation of a logistics audit in this area, especially since the supply chain can be not just a single enterprise but the entire network cooperating on the basis of delivery and receipt of goods. In addition, the flows carried out in these chains may concern not only materials or finished products, but also cash, human and technological resources, and information. The latter can also come both from internal sources and from outside the entire system. What's more, the flows are "driven" by all entities that participate in the supply chain, and whose number can reach up to several units, depending on the length of the chain. The situation becomes even more complicated if it turns out – which is not difficult to imagine from the perspective of the development of modern enterprises – that we are dealing with an international supply chain. In such a case, logistics activities within the supply chain are carried out across and beyond the borders of different countries.[24] At this point, it is important to mention the numerous processes that we deal with in the supply chain, which are also in the circle of interest in auditing and concern (Douglas, 2008):

- customer relationship management,
- supplier relationship management,

- customer service management,
- demand management,
- order fulfillment,
- manufacturing flow management,
- product development and commercialization,
- returns management.

Since the above-mentioned processes are often interrelated, the auditor's identification of the root causes of problems that may arise in these areas may require constant and detailed research.

In conclusion, we can see that the supply chain is a complex and complicated issue that indirectly determines the nature of the logistics audit itself carried out in this field, thus making it difficult to implement. It is also worth noting that due to time or resource constraints, logistics audits of the supply chain usually focus their attention on one selected element, which in turn makes it difficult to obtain a holistic view of the functioning of the entire supply chain in the organization. Due to the fact that nowadays we observe an increase in the complexity of many supply chains, it is likely that we should also expect an increase in the scope and number of logistics audits carried out in this area.

3.6. Control and analytical questions

Control questions

1. Provide a definition of a logistics audit of production and specify its primary and auxiliary purposes.
2. Provide a definition of a logistics audit of a warehouse and present its general objectives.
3. Define the following concepts: distribution, distribution logistics, distribution channel, distribution logistics audit.
4. Name the quantitative and qualitative indicators for evaluating the effectiveness of distribution logistics.
5. Present procurement logistics goals by task and activity.
6. Present the definition and basic objectives of the logistics audit of procurement.
7. Provide a definition of supply chain and logistics audit of the supply chain.
8. Define and define the basic objectives of a logistics audit of the supply chain.
9. Describe the forms that a logistics audit of the supply chain can take.
10. Replace the basic processes taking place in the supply chain.

Analytical questions

1. On the basis of practice, the objectives of the logistics audit of production are implemented with the help of various methods, techniques, and research tools. With this in mind, name three of them and describe how to apply them.
2. In your opinion, how can the organization benefit from the implementation of a logistics audit of the warehouse? Justify your answer.
3. Characterize the areas, along with the type of costs that are generated in them, which may be of interest to the logistics audit of distribution.
4. Present the arguments for the fact that the logistics audit of distribution is an important tool to support the management of the organization in achieving its strategic goals.
5. Why is a logistics audit of the supply chain a type of industry audit, the implementation of which is demanding and often raises many problems? What is it caused by? Justify your answer using appropriate argumentation.

Notes

1 These include all work items that are consumed once and completely in a production cycle. According to the definition used by the Central Statistical Office, materials also include non-durable objects (tangible current assets gradually consumed in the production process), parts of machinery and equipment, useful production waste, as well as packaging.
2 Purchasing in practice boils down to the actual (physical) act of buying goods (service).
3 Independent needs (primary demand) are needs resulting from customer demand for the final goods of the enterprise. It is a demand strongly determined by the market, which is why it is always characterized by a certain level of unpredictability (uncertainty). As for dependent needs (secondary demand), they result from primary demand, the structural structure of the product, as well as the technology used and the organization of production. In practice, this is the demand for materials and other elements needed to produce final products. Importantly, with a specific structure of demand, the demand is determined based on direct calculations and is therefore not subject to any degree of uncertainty.
4 The verification procedure of qualified suppliers implemented in an enterprise should also be analyzed.
5 Product profitability is the ability of a product to generate profit from every dollar obtained from the market. In other words, we consider a profitable product to be a product whose sales revenues exceed its overall costs (including production, marketing, promotion, etc.).
6 TQM is a management technique based on the assumption that all employees of the organization constantly improve their skills and improve their competences in order to achieve maximum customer satisfaction with the products and/or services it offers.

7   It includes the internal movement of raw materials, components and sub-assemblies from warehouse halls, storage points and side production lines to the so-called production cells. Internal logistics also includes transport and picking of ready-to-load products and transport.

8   Quantitative, qualitative, and those bearing the characteristics of a scientific experiment.

9   A process of analyzing large data sets in terms of looking for anomalies, deviations, paradigms, or correlations in order to predict final results based on them.

10   Business analytics, which in practice is an action of transforming data into useful information and knowledge.

11   Key performance indicators (KPIs) are measures by which management can constantly monitor the progress of the organization in achieving the assumed goals, including the implementation of the strategic goal.

12   Krzyżaniak et al. (2014) define the storage process as "operations relating to the temporary receipt, storage, completion, movement, maintenance, recording, inspection and delivery of goods."

13   In the receipt phase, the delivered goods are unloaded and identified, and are then sorted. At the same time, they are inspected both quantitatively and qualitatively. In practice, the acceptance phase is the stage of preparing the goods for their storage. The second phase – storage – involves the receipt of goods from the reception zone and placing them in the storage zone (i.e., the arrangement of the assortment in the warehouse zone). In this zone, the goods are periodically inspected and then issued to the picking area. During the picking phase, stock sets are created according to quantitative and assortment specifications for the defined customer. In other words, at this stage, it is about the preparation of a completed order for the recipient/customer. The final stage of the storage process is the release phase. In this part of the process, the packaged items are formed into transport units and then sent from the warehouse to the specified customers.

14   In the opinion of Brzeziński (2005), logistic potential is a function of logistic capabilities, which are dynamic and time-varying quantities. Thus, their evaluation can only be carried out within a defined time frame under precisely defined conditions that take into account the restrictions existing for a given period of time. The cardinal elements of the logistics potential defined in this way include human potential, material potential, technical potential, and management potential.

15   The essence of heuristic methods, which do not belong to the methods of creation but rather are conducive to creation, is to arrive at original and innovative solutions through discovering new facts, contacts, and relationships taking place in reality. More information on this subject can be found in Martyniuk's book *Introduction to Invention*, second edition, which in 1997 was published by the University Publishing House of the Cracow Academy of Economics (now the Cracow University of Economics).

16   The concept of the value chain was created and popularized by M.E. Porter of Harvard Business School. For more on this topic, see Porter, M.E. (1998). *Competitive Advantage: Creating and Sustaining Superior Performance (With a New Introduction)*, The Free Press, New York.

17   Also called profitability or rate-of-return indicators. They are often used in the evaluation of enterprises. However, their usefulness is largely limited by the fact that they have a high level of generality, which reduces their economic content.

18 From the Latin, *distributio*, meaning division, separation.
19 Peter Thiel, co-founder and investor of the American enterprise PayPal Holdings, Inc., and Elon Musk's business partner, in one of the interviews stated that poor distribution – not the product – is the main cause of an enterprise's market failures.
20 In the opinion of Śliżewska and Zadrożna (2014), the primary task of distribution is to fill the gaps that arise between the sphere of production and consumption, and which concern the time gap, the spatial gap, the quantitative gap, the gap in the assortment, and the information gap.
21 For more on this subject, see Frankowska, M., Jedliński, M. (2011). *Efficiency of the Distribution System.* PWE, 1st ed., Warsaw.
22 Vertical integration of distribution channels consists of linking channel entities located at different levels of distribution by means of contracts, agreements, or economic subordination. Horizontal integration, on the other hand, is a combination of the resources of two or more intermediaries within the same level of distribution who have different competences, when those intermediaries want to use them together on the basis of cooperation and mutual exchange.
23 For more on this topic, see: *Supply Chain Audit Case Study*, http://hafezicapital.com/supply-chain-audit/, [Accessed 14.01.2021].
24 See Gołembska, E. (2007). *Basic Problems of Global Logistics, International logistics, Eurologistics*, Wydawnictwo Naukowe Wyższej Szkoły Kupieckiej, Łódź.

4 Logistics audit

A management approach

4.1. Audit – a tool for improving the organization

As Trenkner (2016) rightly points out, the need for improvement, or, precisely speaking, the need to induce the need for improvement, has been known about for decades. Nowadays, it takes on a special meaning, especially in relation to organizations that need to prepare for digital transformation. Its scale of influence on the current manner of functioning of the world and enterprises is best evidenced by the fact that often in the subject literature, the noun "transformation" is replaced by the term "revolution." Thus, we can risk the thesis that we are currently dealing with a revolution rather than a digital transformation. This distinction seems to be important because in the case of revolution – and unlike transformation – the changes taking place are decisive and rapid rather than transformative. Considering this, and the issues presented further in this chapter, it is therefore necessary to ask ourselves a basic question about the semantic character of the terms "improvement" or "improving." To improve means to take conscious action in order to make something better than before. And so we can improve not only spoken or written language or craftsmanship, but also methods, techniques, structures, systems, or processes. Improving the latter of these elements seems to be particularly close to any modern organization that systematically strives to be more efficient, more effective, or more flexible and thus quickly adapt to the changing environment around them. In general, we can even conclude that an organization's pursuit of excellence[1] (being a role model for others in the market), in all its possible areas and aspects, has become in recent years an *idée fixe* for a significant number of managers. Indirectly, Kozina (2014) also draws attention to this, arguing that the conditions in which modern organizations operate, including a turbulent environment, global dimension of competitiveness, and rapid development of technology, somehow force them to constantly improve management tools in various areas of the company's activity. In this regard, let us note that not

DOI: 10.4324/9781003380184-5

only the organizations themselves are subject to improvement but also the instruments that are used to manage them, including (Wąchol, 2010):

- management concepts – including classical, behavioral, systemic, situational, quantitative, socio-cultural,
- management models – including the rational purpose model, the internal process model, the human relations model, the open systems model, the 7S model,[2]
- management methods – including benchmarking, controlling, lean management, outsourcing, quality management, strategic management, project management, virtual organization, agile organization, innovative organization, process organization, mergers and acquisitions,
- management techniques and management tools – including mathematical, quantitative, qualitative, IT, communication, offensive, system, task-based, comprehensive techniques, e.g., systemic, algorithms, analytical sheets, diagrams, audits.

Among the wide range of tools that are currently used by executives in the process of managing the organization, or more precisely, in the process of its improvement, an audit occupies a special place. In principle, one can put forward the thesis that it is a management instrument that nowadays is not alien to any organization regardless of its size, area, and scope of functioning, as well as the industry in which it operates. Therefore, at this point, the question should be asked: what makes the audit function (especially internal) in an organization so unique? The answer to this question is not so much complex as multithreaded. The point is that the audit – especially an internal audit – can relate to any area of functioning of a given unit. Its scope is virtually unlimited and can also apply to the environment outside the organization. Nevertheless, the importance of the audit against the background of other tools used in the management of the organization is that:

- it provides a holistic approach (holistic and systemic) to assess the state of functioning of the organization,
- it supports and evaluates the management staff in the context of risk management and the correct functioning of the internal control system in the organization,
- it is the third line of defense in risk management and provides an assessment of the processes necessary for the effective functioning of the first and second lines of defense in the organization (see Figure 4.1),
- it provides its main stakeholders with valuable and objective information on the functioning of the organization in terms of financial, operational, managerial, legal, or dealing with risk,

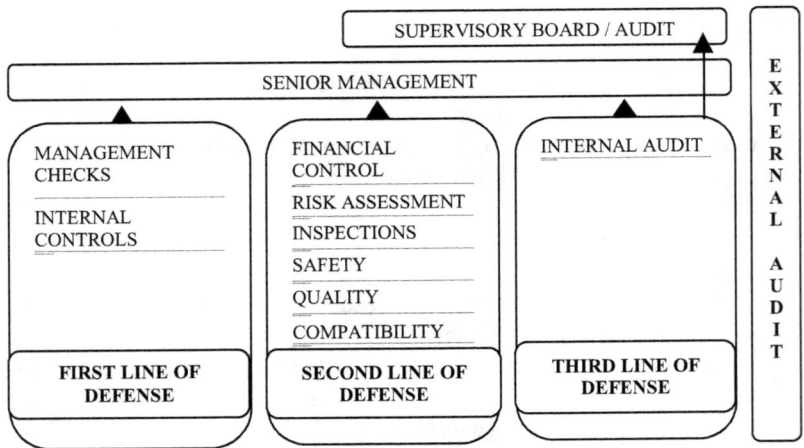

Figure 4.1 Three-line risk defense model from an audit perspective Source: Developed on the basis of the Institute of Internal Auditors.

- it is a provider of advisory services that are designed to improve activities in the organization and contribute to the implementation of its strategic goals.

When taking into account the rare features of the audit compared to other management tools, let us note that through it many areas may be subject to improvement in the organization: financial, technical, operational, as well as organizational, qualitative, or legal issues. What's more – as part of them – both tangible and intangible objects can be improved, which relate directly to (Szczepańska, 2011):

- the organization itself,
- products of the organization's activities (products, services, patents, designs, etc.),
- activities of the organization (work, production, processes),
- elements of the organization (organizational structure, organizational culture, ties, mission, vision, strategic and operational goals),
- relations taking place in the internal and external environment of the organization (relations of the organization with its stakeholders).

The processes of organization improvement carried out as part of the audit may take on various types, which in tabular terms are presented in Table 4.1.

Table 4.1 Improvements – a typology

Criterion	Type of improvement
Durability and continuity	• Continuous (permanent) • Jumping (varied)
Truthfulness (axiological)	• True (real) • Untrue (illusory) • Ethically reprehensible (amoral)
Pattern disclosure	• Standard (with a clearly defined perfect state) • Non-standard (with clearly blurred or default)
Range	• Integrated (holistic, comprehensive) • Disintegrated (fragmentary, sectional)
Reachable	• Unattainable (idealistic) perfection • Achievable (real) perfection

Source: (Skrzypek, 2014, p. 134).

In practical terms, an audit can therefore help an organization to improve and modernize its constituent elements, including:

- atmosphere and organizational culture – by identifying deficiencies and gaps in the assessment of the functioning of a specific culture in the organization, which create the culture: artifacts,[3] value system, principles, norms, views, or behaviors preferred by the organization. Then the audit can take action to strengthen specific behaviors among employees that are close to the values professed in an organization. This approach seems all the more valuable because, in practice, it builds a platform for discussion and dialogue regarding the importance and role of organizational culture in achieving the goals set by the organization, which emerges among employees and between them and management,[4]
- financial and operating results – which in practice may consist of verification of financial statements from previous years. It often happens that errors and weaknesses are then identified, which are revealed in the financial control system of the organization. Thus, audits of performed tasks, or review of completed financial operations, may contribute to increasing the degree of efficiency of both financial results and the operations (processes) themselves,
- internal systems and control mechanisms – mainly due to the fact that the audit does not focus solely on quantifiable and comparable quantities, but also focuses on the general understanding of the systems and control environment that operate in the organization. In this way, deviations in operating systems (accounting, control) are identified, for which instructions can be formulated and proposals for improvements

can be prepared, which will thus contribute to reducing the risk of the business,

- relations with stakeholders – nowadays, due to the high degree of dispersion of shareholders and the growing complexity of integrated supply chains on an international and even global scale, audit may be the only tool that guarantees stakeholders an increase in the degree of transparency of their operations. Audits contribute to increasing the degree of excellence of each organization,
- internal and external security – mainly by examining both technical aspects of network security (firewalls, system construction, algorithm configuration) as well as organizational or human resources security rules. In this type of audits, verification and evaluation, documents regarding both internal and external security procedures, and policies (occurrence of risk factors) applicable in a given organization are also subject to verification and evaluation.

It is understandable that the above-mentioned components of the organization are only a small part of the long list of components that may be subject to effectiveness as a result of the implementation of audit tasks. Nevertheless, the path of implementation of such a process can be both time-consuming and capital-consuming for an organization. What's more, there is no guarantee of success. Paraphrasing Langley et al. (1996), in the context of an integrated approach to process improvement, one can even confirm that any improvement will require change, but not all changes will result in improvement.

In general, regarding the audit approach to organizational improvement presented in this chapter, it should be emphasized that such activities should be defined for different structures and levels of the organization; the more so because these activities properly fit into the concepts of management science, which since its inception – and thus since the birth of the school of scientific management[5] – have placed great emphasis on activities aimed at its improvement. As Cyfert (2006) points out, any omission in the area of organizational improvement, especially in the long term, can lead to serious dysfunctions in the management system, causing the disintegration of processes, procedures, and practices used in the organization.

4.2. Logistics audit in the organization – analysis of the logistics system potential

As part of the managerial assessment of the state of logistics of the enterprise, a logistics audit can also act as a diagnostic tool used to synthetically assess the potential of the entire logistics system. However, the definition of the potential of the logistics system referred to in this book must first be preceded by an explanation of such concepts as analysis, potential, or potential of the system. Therefore, analysis should be understood as a detailed and multi-faceted[6] study of a given phenomenon or problem, the final product of which is the formulation of factual conclusions. As for the word "potential," it is referred to as a resource of possibilities or various types of abilities. In the case of economics, these resources of capabilities, abilities, or performance are most often attributed to given individuals, organizations, groups of people, or systems. As noted by Mastelarz-Kodzs (2018), the size of the potential of a given object or subject can be determined by the set of abilities, competences, skills, and abilities possessed. Not without significance are also qualifications related to the use of these resources, as well as the resources in the environment. Therefore, taking as a criterion the area of occurrence of specific resources of possibilities, we can talk about economic potential, financial potential, market potential, technological potential, or (so popular today) intellectual potential. Having knowledge of what is potential, especially in the context of economic sciences, we can now determine what the potential of the system is.

In this chapter, by potential of the system, we will understand the totality of its possibilities of functioning in accordance with its original purpose. However, it should be mentioned here that the possibilities, capabilities, or resources of the system are not unlimited but are adapted to the given circumstances (boundary conditions). We can now answer the question about the definition of the potential of a logistics system. And so, in broad terms, the potential of the logistics system of the organization can be understood as a force that affects the goals and strategy of the organization. In the case of a narrow approach, we can use the definition proposed by Wasiak (2013), where the potential of the logistics system is understood as its resources and the relations that take place between them, taking into account the principles of work organization, which enable the implementation of specific transformations in the flow of goods and related information. You should be aware that the potential of the organization's logistics system is constantly changing, as a result of changes taking place, for example, among the qualifications and key competences possessed by employees. In addition, as part of a logistics audit, potential can be evaluated using a wide range of measurement methods[7] and techniques related to the overall assessment of the functioning of the logistics system in the organization (see Figure 4.2).

In the context of a holistic assessment of the logistics system, the logistics audit focuses on several important issues:

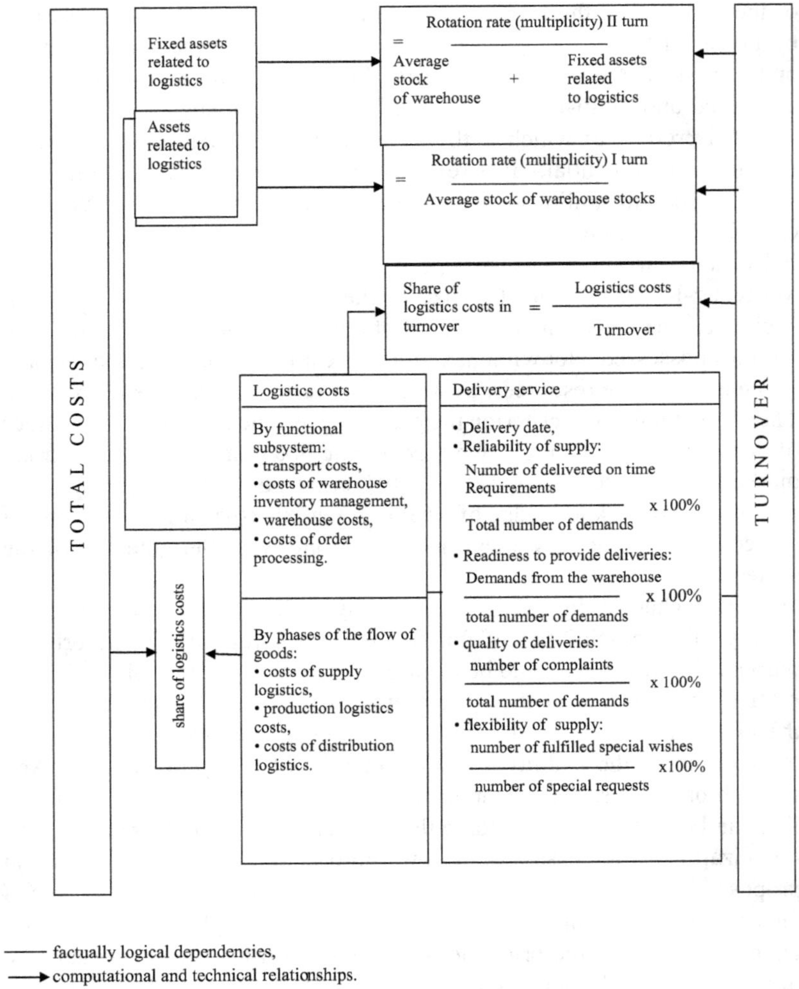
TOTAL COSTS
Fixed assets related to logistics
Assets related to logistics
Rotation rate (multiplicity) II turn = Average stock of warehouse + Fixed assets related to logistics
Rotation rate (multiplicity) I turn = Average stock of warehouse stocks
Share of logistics costs in turnover = Logistics costs / Turnover
Logistics costs
By functional subsystem:
• transport costs,
• costs of warehouse inventory management,
• warehouse costs,
• costs of order processing.
By phases of the flow of goods:
• costs of supply logistics,
• production logistics costs,
• costs of distribution logistics.
share of logistics costs
Delivery service
• Delivery date,
• Reliability of supply:
Number of delivered on time Requirements / Total number of demands x 100%
• Readiness to provide deliveries:
Demands from the warehouse / total number of demands x 100%
• quality of deliveries:
number of complaints / total number of demands x 100%
• flexibility of supply:
number of fulfilled special wishes / number of special requests x100%
TURNOVER
factually logical dependencies,
computational and technical relationships.

Figure 4.2 Holistic assessment of the logistics system – a system of indicators
Source: (Pfohl, 1998, p. 215).

- first, it involves conducting a comparative analysis, which is designed to confront the current state of the logistics system with a set of conditions to be met in a specific organization,
- second, it evaluates the efficiency of the structures and processes of the logistics system, primarily taking into account key processes and

activities that create value, lead time and process costs, involvement of the organization's employees for process improvement and implemented process innovations,

- third, as part of the verification activities, it identifies areas of potential failures and aberrations in the logistics system, in order to improve its quality and systemic efficiency,
- fourth, it creates a management culture based on quality, commitment, and awareness,
- fifth, it provides important information about the logistics system and the existence of potential risk areas.

Bearing in mind the above, in assessing the potential of the company's logistics system, the logistics audit procedure may be helpful, and covers all its most important aspects, and consists of requirements analysis, implementation analysis, process analysis, structure analysis, and comparative analysis (see Table 4.2). In practice, it involves carrying out five stages (Gudehus & Kotzab, 2012):[8]

- in the first stage – requirements analysis aims to define and formulate expectations in the field of logistics services on the part of all stakeholders of the organization. The implementation of this goal is possible mainly thanks to a thorough analysis of available documents and proper assessment of stakeholder requirements. Their capture is made possible by conducting joint interviews with stakeholders, organizing workshops, and creating focus groups, or building prototypes (models, systems, processes). Then, the requirements obtained in this way from our co-operators should be divided into functional, operational, technical, and transitional requirements, in order to be correct in formulating the final conclusions. Finally, all information collected as part of the implementation of individual phases of the requirements analysis must be critically evaluated, due to the need to eliminate those that contradict each other (e.g., demand for better quality of services, for the same money).
- in the second stage – performance analysis examines at what cost, with what efficiency and quality, logistics services are provided. In practice, the results of the conducted research on the efficiency of the logistics system are obtained through data collection, then their transformation and graphic presentation. The data most often comes from profiles, counters, and residual traces of events that have been recorded in the enterprise's logistics system. In contrast, the efficiency of logistics processes, including their quality and productivity, is often assessed using key performance

Table 4.2 Five-stage analysis of the logistics system in the logistics audit

Stage	Type of analysis	Subject of analysis	Problem questions
Stage I	**Requirements analysis**	Conformity requirements	Are the implemented activities consistent with the long-term logistics strategy of the organization?
		Quality requirements	Does the logistics system in the organization ensure the implementation of its strategic, operational, and tactical goals at the level that guarantees the best quality, efficiency and effectiveness?
		Stakeholder requirements	Does the organization have defined needs for the logistics services of its stakeholders?
		Monetary requirements	Does the organization provide services where the relationship is disturbed: more benefits than costs?
		Transformation requirements	What are the possibilities of easy transition from the current state of the organization's logistics system to the planned (new) state?
Stage II	**Performance analysis**	Bottlenecks	Does the organization constantly identify bottlenecks occurring, for example, in the supply chain?
		Where and when tasks are processed	Is the implementation of logistics functions in the organization in accordance with the requirements regarding time, place, and quantity?
		Working time	Is the number of employees employed in the subsystems of the organization's logistics system adequate to the amount of work necessary to be performed?
		Errors and deviations	Are there places in the organization's logistics system where a disproportionate number of errors occur?
		Logistic costs	What logistics costs are generated in the subsystems of the organization's logistics system?

(Continued)

Table 4.2 (Continued)

Stage	Type of analysis	Subject of analysis	Problem questions
Stage III	**Process analysis**	Logistic units	How does the organization of logistics units affect loading in terms of time and finance?
		Master data set	Does the organization have a logistics database and how does it care about their quality?
		Time	Are bottlenecks in the organization identified from the point of view of delivery deadlines?
		Process costs	Does the organization constantly monitor the prices of materials necessary for the production process on the market?
		Stocks	How does an organization control the state and size of its inventory?
		Quality	Does the organization have developed standards and procedures in the field of quality of services provided?
		Process planning and control	How has the scope of work been defined in the organization, for people responsible for planning and controlling logistics processes?
		Supply chain	Have you identified supply chains in your organization that are strategic to your organization?
		Make or Buy (MOB)	Does the organization conduct benchmarking that allows it to solve problems such as: make or buy?
Stage IV	**Structure analysis**	Logistics infrastructure	Is, and how often is, the logistics infrastructure analyzed in the organization in relation to competitors?
		Channels and distribution network	Does the organization identify weak links in distribution channels that are responsible for the movement of tangible and intangible goods?
		Costs of doing business	Are the tasks and the way of organizing work in the organization optimal and does not generate unnecessary costs?

(*Continued*)

Table 4.2 (Continued)

Stage	Type of analysis	Subject of analysis	Problem questions
Stage V	**Comparative analysis**	Benchmarking	How do the organization's results compare to the competition?
		Case studies	What are the strengths and weaknesses of the organization compared to the industry competition?
		Existing data	What conclusions can the organization draw from an in-depth analysis of data from previous periods of activity?

Source: Authors' own study based on: https://logisticaudit.wordpress.com/

indicators. At the same time, what should be emphasized here is that – in narrow terms – the analysis of performance, additionally includes:

- bottleneck analysis, which consists of identifying constraints and then minimizing or eliminating them, in order to improve the efficiency of processes taking place in the logistics system and subsystems of the organization,
- processing times analysis, which is associated with the assessment of the actual state of the order processing-time with the time of stay (the period in which a given item or service stayed in the selected area),
- deadline task analysis, which includes the assessment of the summary of the implementation of specific tasks in terms of defined deadlines. In practice, this type of analysis gives the opportunity to obtain a relatively objective picture related to the generation of additional costs, resulting from exceeding the time of task implementation in selected subsystems of the logistics system,
- error analysis, which consists of documenting (recording) errors that may occur both in relation to the objects being subjected to measurement, may be dictated by the properties of the measurement tool, or may be related to the bias of the person making the measurement. In addition, it is worth adding here that errors in the functioning of the logistics system can be characterized by regularity, randomness, but also excessiveness. A thorough analysis of these errors, however, allows for a precise estimation of the costs they generate in the organization's logistics system,
- cost logistic analysis, which provides information on the location, level, and dynamics of cost formation in various areas and subsystems of the logistics system. Thanks to the information obtained in

this area, the enterprise management can initiate actions aimed at reducing costs, e.g., by launching cost-reduction programs.

- in the third stage – process analysis provides a series of activities whose main goal is to gain understanding in the functioning of all logistics processes taking place in the logistics system of the organization. Knowledge about processes is obtained mainly from reviewing the elements of the process, getting acquainted with its input and output data, checking procedures and control systems, evaluating the applications used, or interacting with other objects and devices. Therefore, when making a holistic assessment of the potential of a given process in a logistics system, the following are taken into account: master data (including data on technological solutions, suppliers, customers, products, services, contracts, locations), time, costs, warehouse inventory, quality and continuous improvement policy, internal and external work organization, process planning and control policy, material and intangible resources of the organization, methods supply-chain management, the possibility of using the "make or buy" method (see Table 4.2),

- in the fourth stage – structure analysis provides the opportunity to assess the existing system structure, from the point of view of the conditions in which it operates. The subject of the analysis of the structure of an object or system may be its level: flexibility, complexity, modernity, centralization, hierarchy, network of connections, and interdependencies, etc.,

- in the fifth stage – comparative analysis allows the identification of differences and similarities occurring in the company's logistics system compared to others on the market. This type of analysis can be carried out using, for example, the benchmarking method.

The above-outlined five-step procedure for analyzing the potential of the logistics system (see: Figure 4.4) enriches the role of the logistics audit in improving the enterprise in general and the logistics system in particular. In addition, it is a comprehensive tool in identifying and removing barriers in the subsystems of the logistics system that limit its ability to implement the process of continuous improvement. In addition, the presented procedure clearly changes the essence of the logistics audit approach to the challenges and problems it faces, from reactive to proactive. As Nogalski and Marcinkiewicz (2004) argue, such an attitude may even be a starting point for the development of a model of proactive and reactive actions, which will be a recipe for crisis situations that the enterprise may face in the future. Therefore, let us note that the scale of the impact of a logistics audit on the organization may, as is often the case, take on a strategic character.

4.3. Logistics audit in the organization – identification of risks in logistics processes

The implementation of a logistics audit in the organization, *ex definitione*, provides it with information both about the possibilities and directions of improving the current situation in which it is located as well as the processes that are implemented in its logistics system. In practice, the auditor, in order to acquire knowledge – especially in the area of logistics processes – subjects an organization to a thorough analysis in terms of quality, efficiency, technology used, the impact of exogenous factors, or susceptibility to changes and the occurrence of crisis situations. However, one of the overarching goals that guide the implementation of a logistics audit is to identify potential threats and risks[9] that may occur within logistics processes. Recognition should be understood not only as the identification of risks, their measurement, or giving them a hierarchy of "importance," but also their quantitative and qualitative estimation, taking into account also – and perhaps above all – the probability of occurrence of a given phenomenon or situation in the future. However, before we move on to the description of the types of risks and issues related to them in the context of logistics processes and logistics audit, let's first refer to the essence and definition of the concept of risk. As noted by Buła (2015b), risk is an interdisciplinary category that can be considered in psychological-sociological, mathematical-statistical, and financial terms. Nevertheless, it is in the social sciences (and especially in economics) that it is the subject of the most numerous applications, approaches, or studies. But, paradoxically, the multifaceted nature of the term determines its complexity, which is emphasized mainly by the number of scientific interpretations and approaches. What's more, one can even put forward the thesis that risk, as a phenomenon, is one of the better described conceptual categories in modern management science, which – despite the passage of time and its popularity – still has the potential for research and scientific development. In dictionary terms, the term "risk," which derives from the Dutch *risico*, or German *risiko*, means an action with unknown effects. As a non-objective category in management science, risk refers mainly to economic, financial, and organizational projects, the result of which is unknown, uncertain, or unpredictable in any way, without the use of the measurement techniques available today. Risk is, which should be clearly emphasized here, a chronic phenomenon, an element that constantly accompanies the organization (see Figure 4.3) and is present in it, at various levels of the organizational structure. In addition, it is a category whose sources of origin can be diverse and multifaceted, which in tabular terms is presented in Table 4.3.

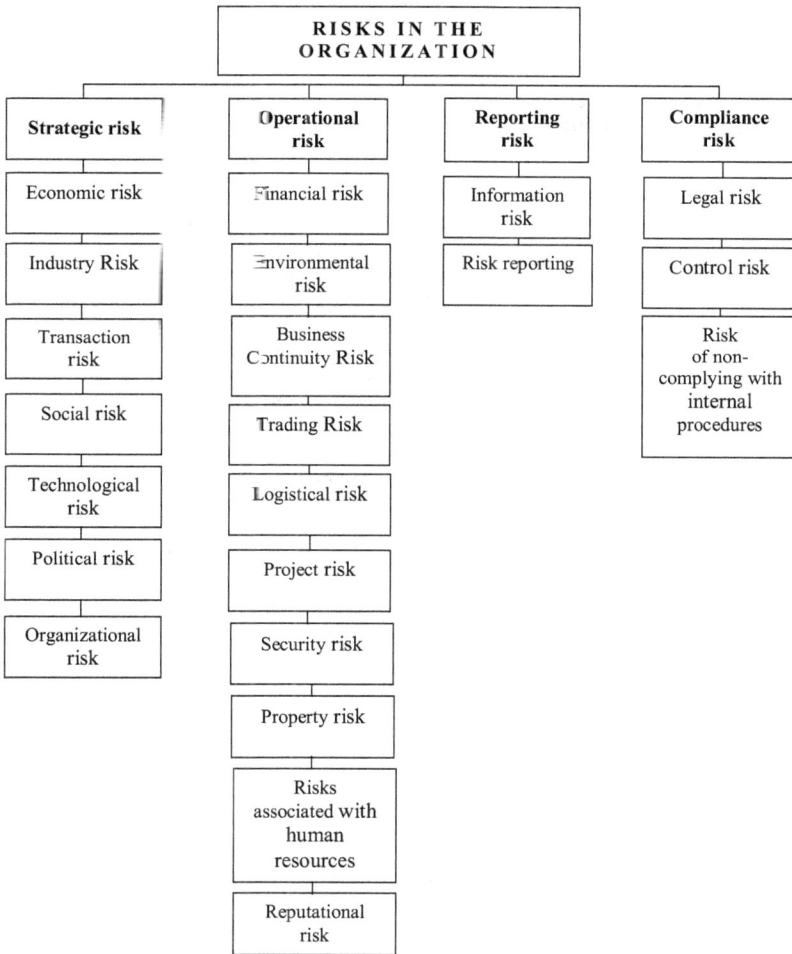

Figure 4.3 Categories and types of risks in the organization Source: Authors' own study based on Bekefi et al. 2008, p. 10.

Thus, it should be stated that the risk always exists, it results from something and something accompanies, increases, or decreases it, and it is an immanent feature of the functioning of any organization. However, if we wanted to define risk in the context of logistics systems, Szymonik (2014) argues that risk is the conditions under which the logistician knows the likelihood of an activity being obtained by a deliberately organized and

Table 4.3 Typology of risks – according to basic criteria

Division criterion	Risk type	Explanation
Formation factors	**External risk**	
	Political	Risk resulting primarily from political changes or political instability (the basic organs of the State) in a given country
	Social	Risk resulting from the belonging of a given person or persons to a specific social group (e.g., religious, cultural, etc.)
	Legal	Risk resulting from the possibility of incurring losses by the organization as a result of instability of legal provisions or their different interpretations
	Interest rate	Risk resulting from the negative impact of changes in market interest rates on the organization's operations, e.g., as a result of banking and insurance contracts concluded by it
	Currency	Risk resulting from the impact of exchange rate fluctuations (increase, decrease) of one currency in relation to another
	Liquidity	Risk associated with the lack of timely implementation of liabilities, due to the different dates of cash inflow and outflow
	Internal risk	
	Management	Risk, which is a consequence of human decisions (intentional and unintentional), having a negative impact on the organization's activities
	Human resources	Risk associated with conducting an improper personnel policy in the field of, for example, recruitment, incentive systems or the scope of responsibility
	Non-compliance	Risk, non-compliance, or violation by the organization of legal provisions or internal regulations, in the form of procedures, standards, recommendations, orders, and regulations
	Corporate	Risk that refers to the obligations and threats facing the organization, related to, for example, IT failures
Repeatability	Systematic	Risk that is caused by general economic factors, most often of a global nature, over which organizations have no influence because they are shaped in a way that is independent of their will or actions taken

(Continued)

Table 4.3 (Continued)

Division criterion	Risk type	Explanation
	Specific	Risk that is individual and is associated with a specific business activity of a person or organization. Its source may be, for example, competition or a specific type of investment
Effect	Pure	Risk that occurs when there is a danger of incurring a loss, without any chance of winning. Most often, this type of risk concerns events of a random nature
	Speculative	Risk that can cause both losses and profits. This is a risk that is taken consciously
Time	Strategic	Long-term risk related to the existence of the organization
	Operating	Short-term risk related to the current functioning of the organization
Variability of the environment	Static	Risk, occurring constantly regardless of technical or economic progress, associated with the occurrence of the forces of nature
	Dynamic	Risk that occurs in connection with continuous technological, economic, economic, and social progress
Impact measurement	Financial	Risk whose impact can be quantified and assessed from the point of view of the financial results of the organization
	Non-financial	Risk whose impact cannot be quantified and assessed from the point of view of the organization's financial results

Source: Authors' own study based on: Młodzik, 2013, pp. 441–442.

combined set of elements (subsystems) such as procurement, production, distribution, together with the relationships between them and their properties conditioning the flow of material and information. Therefore, we can see that, in synthetic terms, the risk in the logistics system is the sum of adverse phenomena or events occurring in the subsystems that make it up, including transport, procurement, storage, production, order fulfillment, distribution, and supply chain. With this in mind, including the topic of this section, we will now move on to defining risks in relation to logistics processes. We will determine the state characterized by the uncertainty of the occurrence of undesirable events in the integrated – in terms of time, costs, and goals – flow of tangible and intangible resources in the organization's business activity, aimed at satisfying the needs of customers. Kuklińska and Koziarska (2017) emphasize that risk in logistics processes appears regardless of the size of the enterprise, its organizational and legal form, the sector or industry in which it operates, as well as its position on the market. Nevertheless, its scope, impact, or frequency of occurrence is largely determined by the prism of the appearance of modern logistic processes, which are characterized by greater dynamics, complexity, or length, as well as susceptibility to endogenous and exogenous factors. Due to the fact that phenomena with unknown effects (read: risks) are gaining strength in logistics processes – both in quantitative and qualitative terms – the role (prestige) of the logistics audit as the tool for their identification and elimination, is also increasing. And although this is not an easy task, a logistics audit can serve as an effective tool in identifying categories, types, or groups of risks occurring in logistics processes. Their numbers and multifaceted nature are presented in Table 4.4.

The above-presented in table 4.3 categories, types, and groups of risks to which enterprises are exposed, as are their logistic systems and processes functioning within them, do not exhaust either their long list or the entire problem that is related to this phenomenon. From the point of view of the enterprise and the elements that make up it, selected risks may disappear (or weaken), and in their place may arise new ones related to the development of the digital economy[10] and, consequently, to digital risk. In practice, enterprises – taking into account the wide spectrum of activities and tasks carried out – should therefore create their own list of risks that are important and critical for their functioning and the business environment. Then, such a risk register should be the subject of the logistics audit, which will examine, assess, and indicate the possibility of adverse events, especially in the area of the organization's logistics system, and recommend a way to eliminate or reduce them.

4.4. The impact of digitalization on the logistics audit

Digitalization is one of the most important megatrends in the world, along with growing migratory flows, the development of a circular economy, cultural convergence, and growing inequalities, or the flourishing of integrated mobility and global supply chains. In practice, the changes it causes (that are often dynamic, but also groundbreaking) with their scope and scale of impact cover both the poor and the rich, developed, and developing countries,[11] as well as all societies and organizations. In view of this, it is not surprising that digitalization is a leading topic of many global events and is the epicenter of scientific interest among researchers and experts. But the important thing is that we are currently only at the beginning of its development. This situation determines several discrepancies and the lack of commonly accepted definitions in science as to terms related not only to digitalization itself, but also to

Table 4.4 Groups of risk in logistics processes

Type of process	Type of logistics processes	Risk groups
Basic processes	Execution of orders (orders) of the client	• Failure to meet the delivery time • Decrease in the number of orders • Defect in the execution of the order
	Implementation of logistic customer service	• Underdevelopment of solutions • Hardware failure • Lack of experience
	Offering additional value to the customer	• Changes in the values offered
	Minimization of costs leading to a reduction in the price of the product and service offer	• Deterioration of quality • Loss of some elite customers
	Receiving and shipping products through the processes of transport, handling, storage, packaging, and marking of products	• Failure to meet the lead time • Decrease in the number of orders • Lack of integration between production, distribution, and transport processes
	Providing the required level of logistical customer service	• Inadequate level of services provided • Insufficiently customer-oriented service process, non-performance of contracts by carriers, logistics operators, etc • Failure of suppliers to comply with technical standards • Quality control system of materials • Punctuality of deliveries
Supporting processes	Analysis and forecast of market logistics situations	• Faulty logistic information system
	Identification of customer preferences and expectations in the field of logistics service	• Problem with identifying key customers or groups of buyers • Inaccurate prediction of customer needs
	Identification of logistic market segments	• Failure to adapt the offer of logistics services to the segment • Lack of integration of all activities related to a given logistics segment
	Development and development of logistics strategies	• Failure to adapt the offer of logistics services to the segment • Lack of integration of all activities related to a given logistics segment
	Development of the set and structure of logistics components mix	• Service-level decisions • Planning of material requirements • Placing orders • Supply forecasting • Location of warehouses and warehouses

(Continued)

Table 4.4 (Continued)

Type of process	Type of logistics processes	Risk groups
	Securing and developing the qualifications of personnel in the field of competence in the design and implementation of logistics processes	• Poor production planning
	Securing the quality of service delivery processes	• Inadequate level of services provided
	Securing the quality of product purchase and sale processes	• Incorrect assessment of the quality of materials • Supplier rating error
		• Incorrect selection of suppliers
		• Faulty quality control assessment of finished products
	Control the flow of products by developing the processes of transport, handling, storage, packaging, and marking of goods	• Lack of internal and external integration in supply chain management
	Issuing instructions regarding the execution of orders and customer orders	• Excessively long time to provide information • Unreadability of information
		• Misinterpretation of commands
	Identification of goals and development of assumptions for the implementation of logistic customer service	• Inadequate ability of partners to respond to unexpected orders (low flexibility, too-slow adaptation to requirements)
Tertiary processes	Securing capacities and potentials for creating added value	• Lack of innovative solutions
		• Lack of implementation of strategies, plans in practice • Limiting oneself to proclaiming slogans (lack of implementation) • The impact of promotion and advertising
	Research and development of logistics infrastructure	• Changes in delivery conditions • Poor production planning • Lack of flexibility in the production process
	Development of information and information technology	• Lack or insufficient flow of information about demand from points of sale and from key customers • Inadequate methods of demand forecasting, problems in the flow of information
	Shaping and maintaining relations and relations with the environment	• Imbalance between customer expectations and the capabilities of all links of the supply chain, misunderstanding of market needs

(*Continued*)

Table 4.4 (Continued)

Type of process	Type of logistics processes	Risk groups
	Management of waste, packaging, permanently damaged products	• Lack of integration with customers • Volatility of demand, relations with contractors • Competitive forces on the market • Market potential • No regulation of waste recirculation • Insufficient environmental awareness • No hazardous waste collection system • No landfills that meet legal requirements • No separate collection of waste
	Securing sales and turnover	• Errors in planning material requirements • Having unnecessary supplies
	Securing the financial aspects of logistics (execution of customer accounts)	• Errors in estimating the customer's profitability • Too-high service costs • Volatility of material prices • Underestimation of projected costs

Source: (Lwowski & Kozłowski, 2007, p. 126).

its close words, such as *digitization* or *digital transformation*. Their source can be both the constant perception of *digitization* in terms of neologisms, as well as ambiguities related to its phenomenon itself. With this in mind, it can be concluded that technology not only changes the language but also often overtakes it. In order to explain how the phenomenon of digitization will affect the implementation of a logistics audit (or audit in general) in an enterprise, we must here – for the sake of clarity of argument and terminological order – define three basic concepts: digitization, digitalization, and digital transformation (see Table 4.5). Apart from the wealth of definitions available in literature, in general terms, digitalization can be understood as a digital (virtual) form of reality. In dictionary terms, digitalization is about using digital technologies to change the existing business model in an organization and provide it with new opportunities to generate revenue and value. The main goal of digitalization is the complete automation of existing operations and business processes of the enterprise. A term close – albeit unequal – to the concept of digitalization is digitization. Łobejko (2018) defines digitization as the process of giving information a digital form. The main goal of digitization, which in fact gave rise to digitization, is to change the document format from analog (not related to computer technology) to digital. Note, then, that what distinguishes the two is that digitization is a "higher" form of digitalization. The only similarity that exists between these concepts is that both digitization and digitalization are processes (systems of successive causally related changes); however, where digitalization should be combined with the process of improvement, digitization should be combined with the process of transformation. The final element of this development process, at the base of which is digitization and at a higher level, digitalization, is digital transformation. In the definition presented by Mazzone (2014), digital transformation is an evolutionary process of a permanent and purposeful nature, which takes place in an organization, which is aimed at its complete digitization (see Table 4.5). This means that digital transformation in the enterprise is subject to the business model, processes,

Table 4.5 Digitalization, digitization, digital transformation – a comparative approach

	Digitalization	Digitization	Digital Transformation
Beginnings of development	1950s	1970s	2000s
Applies to Purpose	Data conversion Changing the format from analog to digital	Data processing Automation of existing operations and business processes	Use of knowledge Changing the organizational culture of the company and the ways in which it acts and thinks
Activity	Convert paper documents, photos, microfilms, LPs*, films and VHS tapes** to digital format	Creating digital work processes	Creating a new digital organization
Tools	Computers and tools for conversion and encoding	IT systems and computer applications	Matrix of new (breakthrough) digital technologies
Challenge	Volume, material	Price, financing	Resistance to changes in human resources
Examples	Scanning of paper registration forms	Electronic registration process	Everything electronic from registration forms to delivered content

Source: Authors' own study based on Savić, 2019, p. 37.
* LP (long play) – vinyl, long playing records. ** VHS (video home system) – a standard for recording video cassettes.

procedures, management methods, as well as relations with customers or employees of the organization. The result of these activities is the creation of a new, digital organization. At this point, however, it should be noted that digital transformation is a serious leadership challenge for those who lead and oversee it. The point is that this type of transformation is aimed at reviving the organization and radically improving its efficiency. The materialization of these aspirations, however, is possible thanks to the skillful use of the potential that lies dormant in global digital technology.

The key factors driving the development of digitization[12] (see Figure 4.4), and thus the creation of the digital economy[13,14] (or *cyber economy*) include primarily (Pieriegud, 2016):

- the Internet of Things, the Internet of Services, and the Internet of Everything,[15]

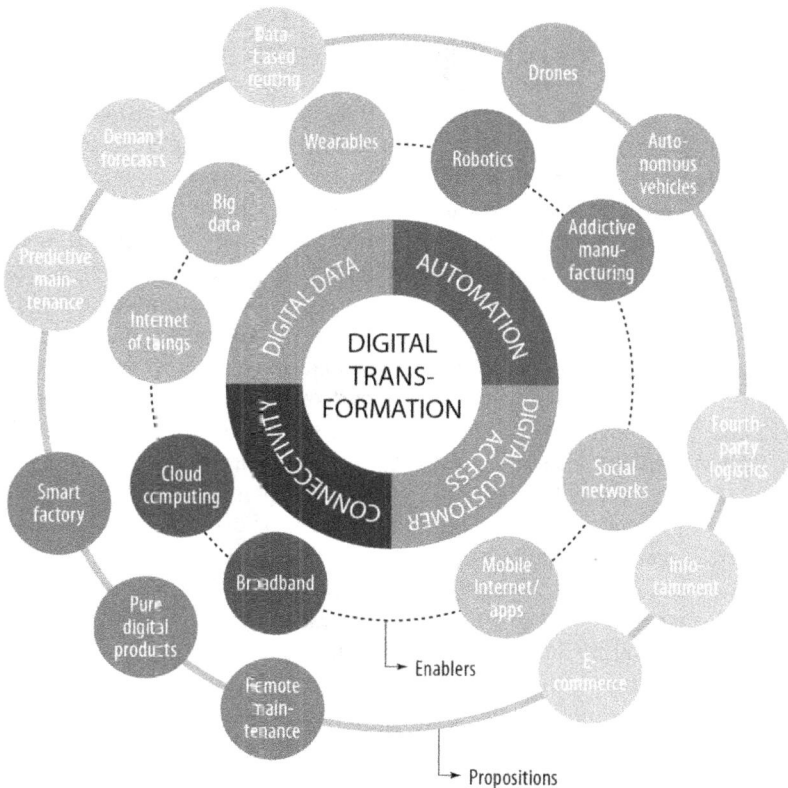

Figure 4.4 Drivers of digitization Source: (Roland Berger, 2015, p. 20).

- ubiquitous connectivity,
- applications and services based on cloud computing,
- big-data analytics and big data as a service,
- automation and robotization,
- multi-channel and omni-channel distribution models of products and services,
- global supply chains.

The consequence of the fact that for nearly two decades the phenomenon of digitization has been accompanying and co-determining the economic development of the world is that some industries have already reached the status of digital maturity. Among them, the most frequently mentioned are telecommunications, technology, media and entertainment, automotive, financial, banking, insurance, manufacturing, or retail trade (Adamczewski, 2018). This group also includes the logistics industry, which is increasingly using digital tools in its activities. For example, one can point to methods of planning inventory volumes, which are increasingly being implemented in this industry using predictive models (predictive analytics). In practice, this means that the growing level of digitization of the enterprise, in a manner previously unseen, transforms the image of, and tools for, the implementation of audit activities. This applies to all types of audits (see Table 1.1), including the logistics audit. Digital technology – including the development of artificial intelligence, data analytics, machine learning, or blockchain[16] – is recomposing the current way of doing business and data analysis, resulting in greater organizational emphasis on data management. From this it also follows that the burden of the organization's interest in verifying and getting to know its customers as part of the Know Your Customer (KYC)[17] procedure will probably soon be shifted toward deeper familiarization, but with current data, this time as part of the Know Your Data (KYD)[18] procedure (Khan, 2018). The question therefore arises as to how the main digital trends (in the form of data analysis or artificial intelligence) will affect the change in the implementation of audit activities and their methodologies. In other words, how will audits face change as a result of the growing global pressure from digital trends (see Table 4.6) or, more broadly, digitization. The answer to this question is not easy, because digitization is not only a massive, multithreaded, and complex phenomenon but, also, one that is not entirely predictable. This, in turn, may have specific consequences both for organizations and for the implementation of the entire audit process. Nevertheless, when trying to answer this question, one should pay attention to several

Table 4.6 Strategic technological trends of the 21st century

Trend	The name of the technological trend	Trend characteristics
Trend 1	Internet of Behaviors (IoB)	In the case of commercial vehicles, behavioral Internet technology can be used in the telematics of transport systems to monitor the behavior of drivers while driving, related to, e.g., sudden braking or making an aggressive turn. Then, the data collected in this way can be used by organizations to improve the efficiency of drivers' working time through better route planning and overall safety improvements. However, this technology can also be used by insurance institutions, especially those who want to monitor the level of physical activity of the insured person, in order to determine their contributions, in the context of their life insurance policy. And such practices can already cause serious ethical or social consequences
Trend 2	Total experience	Holistic experience is the sum of the experiences of all customers, employees, suppliers, users, etc., which is aimed at changing the result of business activity. Its goal is to improve the overall experience in the place where all these elements intersect. Linking all these experiences (as opposed to an individual approach) can serve an organization to differentiate itself from its competitors in a way that is difficult to reproduce, which will be reflected in building a more lasting competitive advantage
Trend 3	Privacy-enhancing computation	Privacy computing is three technologies designed to protect your data as it is used. The first provides a trusted environment in which sensitive data is processed. The second analyzes data in a decentralized manner. And the third encrypts data and algorithms before processing or analyzing them. In practice, this technology allows organizations to securely collaborate in different "configurations" without sacrificing their confidentiality and privacy
Trend 4	Distributed cloud	A distributed cloud (an integrated, multi-cloud world) is a place where cloud services are distributed to various physical locations, with the public cloud provider being responsible for and supervising it. The distributed cloud is considered the future of the cloud services market, due to the fact that the use of a public cloud is cheaper and less complex than in the case of a private cloud. In addition, private clouds are gradually becoming an equal partner for public clouds

(Continued)

Table 4.6 (Continued)

Trend	The name of the technological trend	Trend characteristics
Trend 5	Anywhere operations	A technology and operating model that will enable you to work from anywhere and improve the implementation of business services in a distributed IT infrastructure. Thanks to this solution, owners, employees, customers, or business partners will be able to cooperate and operate physically in remote environments. It is, in other words, a digital enhancement of physical space
Trend 6	Cybersecurity mesh	Cybersecurity mesh is a distributed architectural approach that aims to create a scalable security mechanism that can be quickly adapted to the necessary level of security. As a rule, a cybersecurity network allows users to define a security boundary around the identity of a person or a specific thing
Trend 7	Intelligent composable business	A smart business that is composable is one that can be modified and quickly changed depending on the situation. In practice, digital transformation forces organizations to compose structures, models, and business strategies that will be flexible and have the ability to quickly adapt to changing conditions
Trend 8	AI engineering	A robust AI engineering strategy will facilitate the performance, scalability, interpretability, and reliability of AI models while delivering the full value of your AI investment. It is not uncommon for projects related to artificial intelligence technology to encounter problems in organizations related to their profitability, durability, and management
Trend 9	Hyperautoma-tion	Hyperautomation is a process that involves automating as many business or IT processes as possible, using highly advanced digital tools in the form of artificial intelligence, machine learning, etc. Indirectly, it is driven by those organizations that have older business processes and which (due to changing conditions) need improvement, especially since the efficiency, effectiveness, and business flexibility of processes today determine the market position of many organizations
Trend 10	Blockchain	Blockchain is a blockchain technology (information arranged in blocks) that can be public or private. It is currently a new way of documenting data on the Internet. In practice, it is used to create blockchain applications, such as predictive markets, games, storage platforms, social networks, online stores, etc.

Source: Authors' own study based on Burke, 2020.

important threads and interdependencies between the development of digitization and auditing (including the logistics audit):

- first, the functions that a modern audit has to perform should keep up with the changes that emerge in the area of digital technology. This means that all processes, procedures, and practices carried out as part of audit activities, based on digital technology, must comply with the legal, ethical, and social requirements in the enterprise,
- second, the increase in the number of intelligent organizations forces audit methodologies to seek out and invest in new digital technologies in order to meet the challenges from customers related to the audit service, especially in the area of data analysis,
- third, the rapid growth of data (information) from various sources in organizations, including systems, sensors, databases, or cameras, offers the possibility of conducting a more efficient audit, with higher quality and greater added value for the organization. This is because the new digital tools used in audit – in the form of automated analytical algorithms – provide an opportunity to test entire sets of structured data held by the organization and not, as previously, only its selected, representative samples. Thus, in practice, they eliminate the need to conduct additional audits in the event of unexpected errors,
- fourth, the development of cloud computing[19] technology means that organizations are increasingly processing and storing their data in the cloud. However, access to cloud resources is available not only to employees of the organization but also to third parties. As a consequence, solutions based on cloud computing require auditors to include in their audit tasks additional activities related to the verification of access and functions performed in the context of cybersecurity,
- fifth, companies that currently want to keep up with the dynamically developing and changing organizational environment are beginning, more and more often, to use the knowledge derived from the analysis of large data sets (big data). And although the volume (quantity), velocity, variety, veracity (credibility), as well as the value[20] of these data sets is difficult to process and interpret, they are, at the same time, a valuable source of acquisition of new resources of knowledge about the organization and its environment.[21] However, from the point of view of auditing, the identification and analysis of large data sets can serve as another tool supporting the risk-assessment process in the organization,
- sixth, the growing prevalence of digital tools will foster the dynamic development of remote audits, which can be performed from anywhere in the world and will not require the physical presence of an auditor in the organization (parent or client). In addition, audit activities, such as

the review of documents or interviews, will increasingly be carried out in real time, using the most modern ICT solutions,

- seventh, the ongoing changes will force organizations providing internal audit services (including industry audits) and external audit to find a quick answer to the question of how to audit innovative technologies, whether in the form of intelligent machines, robots, or processes, while taking into account audit quality, the time and costs of its implementation, and applicable laws (Meuldijk, 2017),

- eighth, digitization will necessitate the development of digital skills. A key role in this process will be played by both sectoral schools and universities,[22] which must ensure that this type of qualification is developed among societies. Thus, those education systems that have so far considered thematic areas such as cybernetics or algorithmics as niche, will become outdated. Digital competences, in particular, will be required in the audit profession, both in terms of expertise in auditing intelligent systems, processes, or entire enterprises, as well as the rapid development of remote audits,

- ninth, the evolution of digital technologies will undermine the current value of audit services. So far, the costs of the audit have been largely dependent on the time required for its implementation, but now, thanks to technology, it will be significantly shortened, and thus the fees for audit services will be based primarily on knowledge, support, and the ability to combine them with the enterprise's strategy. In other words, a good audit and its value will depend in the future on the ability to anticipate changes so that the customer can be offered appropriate recommendations and support services,

- tenth, organizations (individuals) providing audit services (including industry audits, including the logistics audit) must invest in the recruitment of digital talent, in cooperation with experts and specialists in the field of digitization and digitization, in artificial intelligence technology and blockchain, in big-data analytics, and cybersecurity. Only then will they be able to deal with the potential challenges and threats that their customers, business partners, or stakeholders will also face.

Finally, it should be noted that the pace and strength of impact from new digital technologies on the audit area (see Figure 4.5) is – in the history of its development – unprecedented and multifaceted. Therefore, in the coming decades, Audit 4.0 will strongly evolve toward the development of Audit 5.0, which will be not only computerized but, above all, remote and digital (see Figures 1.2 and 4.5). In addition, its current reputation – developed

Figure 4.5 Trends determining the development of Audit 5.0 Source: Authors' own study.

over recent years – will require revitalization, due to the fact that the audit will have to face a postmodern reality that will be unprecedented in terms of challenges and changes.

Thus, how the audit will cope with the new digital reality will in the future determine its market position and the value it will represent for enterprises. This task will not be easy, because the audit will have to deal with issues such as digital transformation, investments in new digital technologies, recruitment of people with digital skills, remodeling of existing ways of carrying out audit activities, adaptation to the requirements of digital law (digital rights), launching new forms of communication with stakeholders, and generating business insights anticipating future, possible events (also in relation to various types of risks).

4.5. The current Polish and European market for logistics audit services

The logistics services market in Poland began to develop at the beginning of the 1990s, which was a direct consequence of changes related to its economic and political transformation. In practice, this was reflected in the fact that the centrally planned economy ceased to exist, and in its place a free market and economic freedom were created. These circumstances, with the systematically growing involvement of foreign capital in Poland (in the form of foreign direct investment (FDI) inflow – see Figure 4.6), led to an increase in aggregate demand and the gradual development of the transport, shipping, and logistics (TSL) sector.

Currently, the logistics industry is one of the most important branches of the Polish economy, which in terms of size also stands out among European nations. Despite the global COVID-19 pandemic, further prospects for its development are also promising and the dynamics of economic growth in Poland, even in the situation of its slowdown in Western European countries, will continue to be stimulated even in 2023 through (PwC, 2019):

- a large and absorbent internal market and the further enrichment of society, which in practice will contribute to an increase in consumer demand,

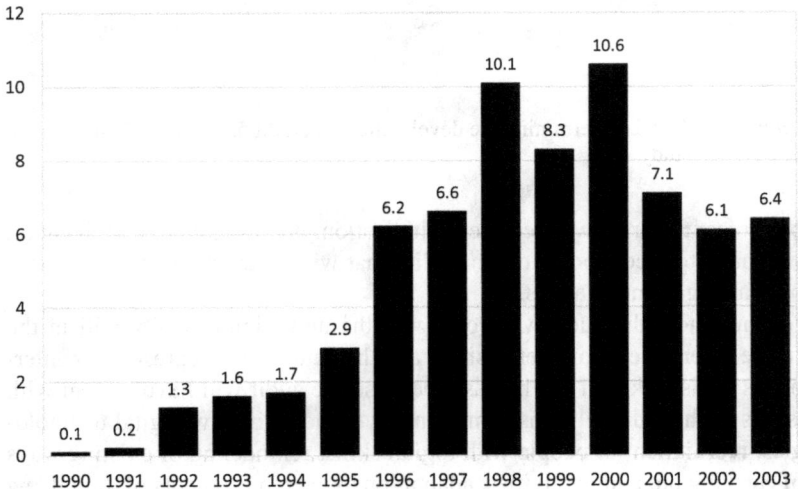

Figure 4.6 Inflow of foreign direct investment into Poland, 1990–2003 (in USD billion) Source: Authors' own study based on Polish Investment and Trade Agency.

- further inflows of EU funds, which will stimulate the level of national investment,
- continued lower labor costs compared to Western European countries (including Germany, France, Belgium, or the Netherlands),
- attractive location of Poland, which therefore draws in foreign investments in industrial plants and distribution centers,
- a well-organized institutional system, especially compared to other countries in Central and Eastern Europe.

Nevertheless, a possible slowdown in economic growth in the rest of Europe should not have a significant impact on the European logistics market, which, according to specialists, is expected to increase by an additional USD 217 billion during 2020–2024.[23] The source of such optimistic forecasts for the logistics industry – despite the COVID-19 pandemic – is the growing number of mergers and acquisitions across the world and a significant increase in global demand in e-commerce, which is expected to reach more than USD 6.5 trillion by 2023. If these forecasts are confirmed, it will mean that in just one decade the level of e-commerce sales on a global scale has increased by over 610% (see Figure 4.7).

Optimistic scenarios for the development of the logistics services market in Poland and Europe, however, should not obscure the challenges faced by

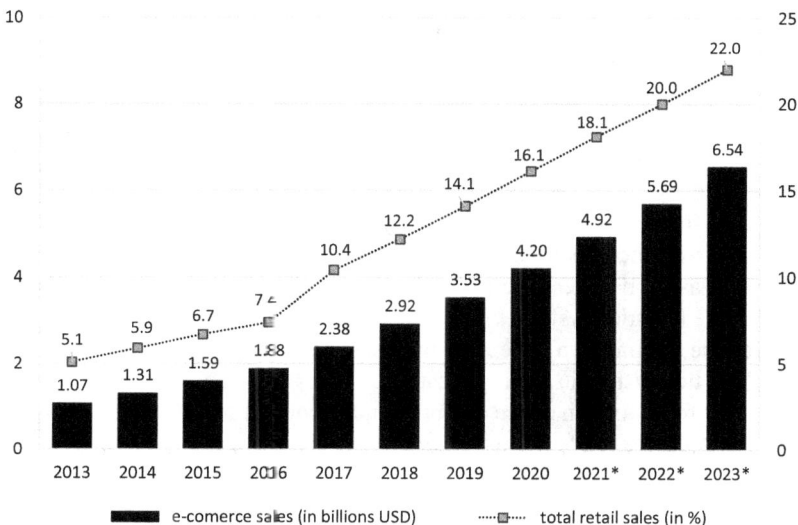

Figure 4.7 Global level of e-commerce sales, 2013–2023 forecast Source: Own study based on eMarketer, Dec 2014 and May 2019.

the industry in the light of the transformation taking place today. It is primarily about the geometrically advancing digitization and the lack of people on the labor market with specific competences, especially given that, in the next two to three years, technologies such as artificial intelligence, IoT, big data, or DLT[24] technology will reach maturity, allowing for a wider use of software (applications), not only in logistics, but also in many other industries (PwC, 2019). In view of the above, it should therefore be expected that, with the further development of the logistics services sector, there will also be a proportional increase in the demand for logistics audit services. In order to improve their efficiency and competitiveness, enterprises will be forced by digital transformation to remodel their existing activities, strategies, and management methods. In this situation, the logistics audit, as a consulting service, can become an indispensable support tool, not only in the context of assessing the state of logistics and improving the functioning of enterprise logistics system but also in the transformation of the current business model into a more "pro-digital" one. In other words, a logistics audit may be necessary to eliminate the organizational dysfunctions of a given enterprise and help to optimize its business strategy; all the more so because, in fact, it is related to the logistics strategy, which in turn is related to the logistics audit.

Nevertheless, current global megatrends alone do not affect the need to decide to conduct a logistics audit in the organization. In practice, the desire to implement such an audit can be triggered by other forces:

- need to improve management activities focused on production, warehousing, transport, distribution, or supply chain,
- assessment of the degree of competitiveness of the organization against the market, in order to implement an effective management strategy,
- decrease in the efficiency of the functioning of certain subsystems such as the logistics system of the organization,
- growing problems in the scalability of business, due to issues related to the costs and expenses of the organization,
- increasing number of errors, difficulties, dysfunctions, or bottlenecks in the logistics system,
- desire to make an independent assessment of the functioning of the logistics system in the organization,
- need for valuation of the company in the context of the implementation of processes related to its merger or acquisition,
- reorganization of internal processes and implementation of new logistics processes.

The management team's decision to carry out a logistics audit in the enterprise entails the need to take another decision related to the form in which it will be carried out. In this case, the issue is whether the logistics audit will be carried out using the internal resources of the enterprise or with the participation of an external entity. The consequence of choosing the second option is that it carries certain risks related to, for example, access by third parties to the company's information, which may be characterized by different levels of sensitivity. Therefore, in order to limit these risks, it is necessary to make a market-based decision regarding the selection of a logistics audit provider, which will take into account issues related to:

- first, comprehensiveness of the audit conducted by the auditor, taking into account and analyzing the cause-and-effect activities (a small change in one subsystem of the company's logistics system may affect both its other elements and the entire system),
- second, the qualifications, experience, and references possessed by the auditor(s), which should coincide with the problem areas occurring in the organization commissioning the audit,
- third, customization of services provided, which will not be of a mass nature but will be tailored to the specific needs and requirements of customers commissioning the implementation of logistics audit services,
- fourth, costs of conducting a logistic audit together with other conditions contained in the commercial contract for its realization.

Bearing in mind the above, we can see that the process of selecting an external entity providing logistics audit services to a given enterprise is not a simple task. It often has a multi-stage character and is subject to various analyses, which ultimately should offer confidence to enterprise management about the correctness of the choice made. Nowadays, on the Polish and European markets, there are various enterprises or institutes that specialize in conducting logistics audits for both private and public business entities (see Table 4.7). Their number is increasing year on year.

On the one hand, this growth is due to the development of logistics and the logistics services market itself, which, in practice, leads to an increase in the number of entities operating within it; and, on the other hand, to the growing demand for audit and logistics consulting services. It should be noted that the entities operating on the market, in addition to logistics audit services, also offer other services in the form of logistics consulting, design of logistics systems, automation of logistics processes (including storage, production, distribution, or supply-chain processes), implementation of e-logistics solutions, and design of logistics systems based on artificial intelligence. Nevertheless, it is the logistics audit that is the service that is most often chosen by enterprises and implemented in various areas of the logistics system. As a result, the following are commonly debated

Table 4.7 Polish providers of consultancy services in logistics audit

Enterprise	Scope of activity
OPTIDATA	The company was founded in 2002, specializing in providing comprehensive solutions for production logistics. This barcode systems or RFID technology supporting production, warehouse, and transport processes. It provides logistics audit services in areas related mainly to storage, production, and transport. It employs people specializing in WMS* and TMS** systems
CHAINGERS	The company was founded in 2005, and is one of the leaders on the Polish market in the field of logistics consulting. It specializes in providing services in the field of logistics audit (in the areas of production, warehousing, supply chain, distribution network, logistics system, and enterprise), logistics strategies, process automation, logistics optimization, warehouse design, and logistics project management. The company's offer is used by the following industries: construction, FMCG***, automotive, electrotechnical, chemical, pharmaceutical, printing, production, tourism, advertising, logistics, and forwarding
ASPECT	Founded in 2002, the company is engaged in the analysis and optimization of the logistics infrastructure of the organization. It provides logistics audit services in the areas of storage, production, and distribution networks. It specializes in the implementation of quick controls. The company's offer is used by the following industries: footwear, forwarding, household appliances/electronics, and furniture
LOGIFACT LOGISTICS SYSTEMS	The beginnings of the company date back to 1999. Since its inception, it has been focused on the design and implementation of WMS. In addition, it is focused on supporting warehouse logistics at the level of operational management. Its portfolio includes over 150 implementations of WMS systems, on both the Polish and the international markets. The company's offer in the field of consulting services includes logistics consulting, logistics optimization for the warehouse management area, and logistics audit
ELANDIS	Founded in Krakow in 2012, the company, from the beginning of its activity, has focused on providing consulting and design services in the area of the supply chain. It provides services in the field of logistics audit of production, warehouse, and distribution. Through its dynamic development and professionalism in the provision of services, the company aspires to the role of an authority in the field of logistics consulting services on the domestic and foreign markets

(*Continued*)

Table 4.7 (Continued)

Enterprise	Scope of activity
ŁUKASIEWICZ RESEARCH NETWORK – INSTITUTE OF LOGISTICS AND WAREHOUSING	The Network is a market-oriented research and development unit, performing the functions of the Polish competence center in logistics and e-economy. The Institute was founded in 1967 and since 1 April 2019 has been part of the Łukasiewicz Research Network. In addition to conducting research, the institute also provides services to external private entities in the field of audit of logistics processes

Source: Authors' own study
*WMS – warehouse management systems. **TMS – transportation management system. ***FMCG – fast moving consumer goods.

procedures: logistics audit of procurement, logistics audit of the warehouse, logistics audit of production, logistics audit of distribution, logistics audit of the supply chain, etc. Finally, it should be emphasized that a competently conducted logistics audit will be an important element of support for the enterprise, primarily by assessing the extent to which its logistics system achieves economic efficiency, effectiveness, and economy.

4.6. Control and analytical questions

Control questions

1. Detail the four tasks on which the logistics audit focuses as part of the overall assessment of the logistics system.
2. What is the performance analysis in the five-stage assessment of the potential of the enterprise's logistics system?
3. Present the types and types of risks that occur in the enterprise.
4. Define the risks that occur in basic logistics processes.
5. Provide a definition of digitization and digitization, and then determine the difference between these conceptual categories.
6. Identify the key drivers of digitalization.
7. What do the acronyms KYC and KYD mean?
8. What is hyperautomation?
9. Name the five trends that determine the development of Audit 5.0.
10. What factors can influence the development of the logistics audit services market in Poland?

Analytical questions

1. Is it right that audit is considered a tool for improving the enterprise? If so, why? What other management instruments do you think

can be subject to the improvement process as part of the functioning of the enterprise?

2. List and briefly characterize the groups of risks occurring in logistics processes, divided into basic, supporting, and tertiary processes.
3. In your opinion, how do the phenomena of digitization, digitalization, and digital transformation affect the development and implementation of the audit? Identify the benefits and risks of these processes for an enterprise.
4. How will hyperautomation and artificial intelligence affect the further development of auditing, including the logistics audit? How will Audit 5.0 (fifth generation) differ from Audit 4.0 (fourth generation)?
5. How do you assess the prospects for the development of the logistics consulting services market, including logistics audit, in Poland? Taking into account the importance of the logistics sector for the Polish economy, do you think that Poland has a chance to become a leader in the provision of logistics audit services in Europe?

Notes

1 Meanwhile, an organization's pursuit of excellence can also be dangerous, especially in situations where management is constantly striving to achieve unrealistic goals and building a dangerous sense among employees that higher-level values in the organization are only perceived in terms of productivity, efficiency, and purposefulness.
2 A model developed by the global consulting firm McKinsey & Company, where the acronym 7S stands for: strategy, systems, structure, shared values, skills, styles, staff.
3 These are products, in the form of a material object, a plan, technology, or language, which are the work of the human mind and human labor.
4 For more on this, see Testa and Sipe, 2013.
5 It was established at the end of the 19th and the beginning of the 20th centuries.
6 The word "analysis" comes from the Greek word *anàlysis*, meaning "disassembly into parts."
7 For more on this topic, see Twaróg, 2003.
8 See: https://logisticaudit.wordpress.com/
9 Extremely often, especially in everyday speech and journalistic writing, the words "threat" and "risk" are treated as if they are synonymous. Meanwhile, threat is something potentially harmful, while risk is, in fact, the probability of a harmful hazard occurring. In order to better understand the difference between these words, we can use the following example, namely: if we are standing on the beach and watching a swimming shark in the sea, it is the shark in the sea that poses a threat to us, while if we swim in the sea, where sharks also swim, then swimming with sharks is a risk for us, associated with, for example, the loss of life.
10 Referred to in Section 4.4.

11 As an example, use the Global Innovation Index 2020 report (*Global Innovation Index 2020*, GII 2020), which also includes a ranking of the ten most innovative countries of 2020, from the group of low-income economies. It included Tanzania, Rwanda, Nepal, Tajikistan, Uganda, and Burkina Faso. For more on this, see Dutta, et al., 2020.

12 As *argumentum a contrario*, several factors can be pointed out that limit the development of digitization, and which have been characterized in detail – in the form of paradoxes. including strategic, supply chain, talent, innovation, and the physical-digital-physical loop – in a report published in 2018 by Deloitte: *The Industry 4.0 Paradox: Overcoming Disconnects on the Path to Digital Transformation (Deloitte, 2018)*.

13 For more on this topic, see Śledziewska and Włoch, 2020.

14 Digital economy is a term used by Don Tapscott. For more on this, see Tapscott, 1998.

15 For more on this, see Section 1.3.

16 Blockchain. in the real world, appeared at the turn of 2016/2017. In a computer network, it is based on a P2P communication model (peer-to-peer, each with each), which means that each user has the same, i.e., equivalent, permissions. Blockchain is a distributed ledger (database) technology that is used to globally record information or a large number of servers and that can be operated simultaneously by many entities in near real time. Its appearance has permanently revolutionized the way various types of records are created, stored, and updated.

17 A due diligence procedure, most often used – but not only – in financial institutions, which allows proper verification of the identity of a given customer.

18 It is a procedure for identifying, verifying, and reviewing data held by an organization, which aims to better understand and understand it. Some types of information at an organization's disposal can serve all stakeholders, while others must remain for its private insight.

19 See Section 2.5.

20 5V symbol – used in characterizing the big-data environment.

21 The Gartner Research Institute (www.gartner.com) reports that by 2021, nearly 80% of business processes in organizations had been modernized and adapted to the requirements related to big data.

22 For more on this, see Jørgensen, 2019.

23 For more on this topic, see *Logistics Market in Europe 2020-2024*, TechNavio, May 2020.

24 Distributed ledger technology (DLT) is a distributed database that is not located in one place but is distributed among a large number of computers on the network. Its members – depending on the permissions granted to them - have both the ability to download and upload data.

Conclusion

The logistics audit is a new and relatively little-described issue in the scientific literature devoted to management, as well as to general audit. A good exemplification of this statement may be the fact that the bibliometric analysis carried out by the authors during the writing of this book – based on the Web of Science (WoS) and Scopus databases – showed that the number of scientific (peer-reviewed) articles containing the phrase "logistics audit" did not exceed 32 in total. What's more, as many as five articles referring to the subject of logistics audit were published only in 2020, while the rest fell in earlier years. However, a clearly greater "wealth" of publications related to logistics audit can be observed in the Google Scholar database. Nevertheless, it is a tool that to this day causes a lot of controversy and gives rise to a lot of divisions in the academic community when it comes to its quality and scientific credibility. However, apart from this, we can conclude, without a shadow of a doubt, that the current knowledge about logistics audit is mainly within journalism publications rather than the scientific literature. It is industry reports, journalistic articles, or specialized Internet blogs, which are often run by people professionally involved in logistics consulting, that provide us with knowledge about what it is, how it works, how it is carried out, and what value this type of audit brings to the organization. Therefore, the knowledge accumulated in this way should become the subject of in-depth analysis by researchers interested not only in the issue of logistics audit or logistics, but also in many other related fields and disciplines. Taking into account the above analysis, the authors believe that the contents of this book will make an important contribution to the development of scientific knowledge about the logistics audit, and internal audit in general, and that they will also meet with a favorable reception from practitioners; particularly because combining scientific knowledge with practice allows for the permanent development of competences, which, in the field of business – but also of science – are considered a *sine qua non* for professional success.

References

Abt, S. (1998). *Zarządzanie logistyczne w przedsiębiorst wie*. Warszawa: Polskie Wydawnictwo Ekonomiczne.

Adamczewski, P. (2018). Ku dojrzałości cyfrowej organizacji inteligentnych. *Studia i Prace Kolegium Zarządzania i Finansów SGH, Zeszyt Naukowy, 161*. Warszawa: Oficyna Wydawnicza SGH.

Adamiecki, K. (1985). *O nauce organizacji*. Warszawa: Polskie Wydawnictwo Ekonomiczne.

Aliyu, A. U. L. (2019). Factors responsible for low productivity in an organization. *International Journal of Economics and Business, 3*(2), ISSN: 2717–3151, LIGS University Hawaii, USA.

Altkorn, J. (2004). *Podstawy marketingu*. Kraków: Instytut Marketingu.

Andjelkovic, A., & Radosavljevic, M. (2020). The length of the distribution channel as a factor of its efficiency. *Strategic Management, 25*(2), 9–017. https://doi.org /10.5937/ StraMan2002009A.

Anthony, R. N., Dearden, J., & Bedford, N. M. (1989). *Management control systems*. Homewood: Irwin.

Antoszkiewicz, J. D. (1999). *Metody heurystyczne. Twórcze rozwiązywanie problemów*. Warszawa: Wydawnictwo Poltext.

Arnold, J., Chapman, S., & Clive, L. (2008). *Introduction to materials management*, wyd. 6. Upper Saddle River, NJ: Pearson Education.

Barcik, R., & Jakubiec, M. (2011). Systemy logistyczne – podstawy funkcjonowania. *Logistyka, 4*, 74–79.

Bartholdi, J. J., & Hackman, S. T. (2006). *Warehouse and distribution science*. www .wareho-. Retrieved from use-science.com.

Bekefi, T., Epstein, J. M., & Yuthas, K. (2008). *Managing opportunities and risks. Management accounting guidelines*. The Society of Management Accountants of Canada, The American Institute of Certified Public Accountants and The Chartered Institute of Management Accountants, Mississaug–New York–London.

Bielińska-Dusza, E. (2009). Identyfikacja problemów badawczych w audycie wewnętrznym. *Zeszyty Naukowe Uniwersytetu Szczecińskiego. Studia i Prace Wydziału Nauk Ekonomicznych i Zarządzania, 16*, 21–35.

Bielińska-Dusza, E. (2011). Funkcjonowanie kontroli zarządczej w systemie kontroli w systemie kontroli wewnętrznej przedsiębiorstwa. *Zeszyty Naukowe Uniwersytetu Szczecińskiego, 669*, 33–48.

Blaik, P. (2001). *Logistyka. Koncepcja zintegrowanego zarządzania.* Warszawa: Polskie Wydawnictwo Ekonomiczne.

Brzeziński, M. (2005). *Logistyka wojskowa.* Dom Wydawniczy. Warszawa: Bellona.

Buła, P. (2015a). *System zarządzania ryzykiem w przedsiębiorstwie, jako element nadzoru korporacyjnego.* Kraków: Wydawnictwo Uniwersytetu Jagiellońskiego.

Buła, P. (2015b). The role of internal audit within corporate risk management viewed from the perspective of corporate governance function. In J. Teczke, K. Djakelii & P. Buła (Eds.), *Management science during destabilization: Local insight* (pp. 285–291). Cracow–Tbilisi: Cracow Univeristy of Economics.

Buła, P., & Niedzielski. B. (2021). *Management, organisations and artificial intelligence. Where theory meets practice.* London: Routledge.

Burke, B. (2020). *Top strategic technology trends for 2021.* Gartner, eBook, Stamfod USA.

Cambalikova, A., & Misun, J. (2017). *The importance of control in managerial work.* International Conference Socio-Economic Perspectives in the Age of XXI century Globalization (pp. 218–229). University of Tirana, Faculty of Economy, Department of Economics, Tirana.

Chow, D., & Heaver, T. (1999). *Logistics strategies for North America* (3rd ed.). Global Logistics and Distribution Planning, Routledge, New York.

Costello, P. J. (2003). Auditing concepts and standards. *NPMA, 15*(6). Atlanta, 12–14.

Cyfert, S. (2006). *Strategiczne doskonalenie architektury procesów w zarządzaniu przedsiębiorstwem.* Poznań: Wydawnictwo Akademii Ekonomicznej w Poznaniu.

Czachorowski, S. (2010). Między ewolucjonizmem a kreacjonizmem – model maszyny i model organizmu. In E. Wiszowaty & K. Parzych-Blakiewicz (Eds.), *Teoria ewolucji a wiara chrześcijan* (s. 60–78). Olsztyn: Wydawnictwo Uniwersytetu Warmińsko-Mazurskiego w Olsztynie.

Dai, J., & Vasarhelyi, M. A. (2016). Imagineering audit 4.0. *Journal of Emerging Technologies in Accounting, 13*(1), 1–15.

De Koster, R. B. M., & Smidts, A. (2013). Organizing warehouse management. *International Journal of Operations and Production Management, 33*(9). https://doi.org/10.1108/ IJOPM-12-2011-0471.

Deloitte. (2018). *The industry 4.0 paradox overcoming disconnects on the path to digital transformation.* Deloitte Touche Tohmatsu Limited.

Dendera-Gruszka, M. Kulińska, E., & Masłowski, D. (2017). Budowa rejestru ryzyka z wy- korzystaniem audytu logistycznego. *Przedsiębiorczość i Zarządzanie,* Wydawnictwo SAN, ISSN 2543-8190, t. XVIII, z. 8, cz. 2, Łódź–Warszawa.

Domschke, W., & Schild, B. (1994). Standortentscheidungen in Distributionssystemen. In H. von Isermann (Ed.), *Logistik – Beschaffung, Produktion, Distribution.* Landsberg am Lech, Köln.

Douglas, M. L. (2008). *An executive summay of supply chain management: Processes, partnerships, performance.* Sarasota, FL: Supply Chain Management Institute, San Diego.

Duda, S. (1997). Typy produkcji w koncepcji Władysława Zawadzkiego. *Annales Universitatis Mariae Curie-Skłodowska, Sectio H, Oeconomia, 31,* 25–49.

Dutta, S., Lanvin, B., & Wunsch-Vincent, S. (2020). *The global innovation index 2020: Who will finance innovation?* NY: Cornell University, INSEAD, World Intellectual Property Organization.

Emerald Publishing Limited. (1988). How do we monitor and report on logistics systems performance? *International Journal of Physical Distribution & Materials Management, 18*(2–3), 78–82. https://doi.org/10.1108/eb014691.

Gary, I., & Manson, S. (2008). *The audit process: Principles, practice and cases* (4th ed.). London: Thomson Learning.

Gattorna, J., Day, A., & Hargreaves, J. (1991). Effective logistics management, *Logistics Information Management, 4*(2). MCB University Press Limited, 2–86.

Gołembska, E. (2007a). *Kompendium wiedzy o logistyce.* Warszawa: Polskie Wydawnictwo Ekonomiczne.

Gołembska, E. (2007b). *Podstawowe problemy logistyki globalnej, międzynarodowej, eurologistyki.* Łódź: Wydawnictwo Naukowe Wyższej Szkoły Kupieckiej.

Gołembska, E. (2010). *Kompendium wiedzy o logistyce* (4th ed.). Warszawa: Wydawnictwo Naukowe PWN.

Gudehus, T., & Kotzab, H. (2012). *Comprehensive logistics.* Berlin–Heidelberg: Springer–Verlag.

Handfield, R. (2020). *What is supply chain management (SCM)?* Raleigh: NC State University.

Handfield, R. B., & Nicols, Jr. E. L., (2002). *Supply chain redesign.* NJ: Prentice Hall, Upper Saddle River, NJ, USA.

Herath, S. K. (2007). A framework for management control research. *Journal of Management Development, 26*(9), 895–915.

Hermanson, D. R., Ivancevich, D. M., & Ivancevich, S. H. (2008). Building an effective internal audit function: Learning from SOX Section 404 reports. *Review of Business, 28*(2), 13–28.

Hochmuth, Ch. A., Bartodziej, Ch., & Schwägler, C. (2017). *Industry 4.0: Is your ERP system ready for digital era?.* https://doi.org/10.13140/RG.2.2.17725.08169.

Ionescu, L. (2010). Exercitarea controlului intern în conditiile crizei economice internationale, Contabilitatea. *expertiza si auditul afacerilor,* nr 8, 55.

Jenkins, B. (1992). *Different types of audits. Environmental auditing in South Australia: Costs and benefits.* https://doi.org/10.13140/RG.2.2.23066.26560.

Jezierski, A. (2007a). Audyt logistyczny w procesach gospodarczych (cz. 1). *Logistyka, 5,* 91–93.

Jezierski, A. (2007b). Audyt logistyczny w procesach gospodarczych (cz. 2). *Logistyka, 6,* 79–82.

Jørgensen, T. (2019). *Digital skills. Where universities matter. Learning and teaching paper #7.* Brussels–Geneva: European University Association.

Kaczmarek, B. (2016). Problemy w organizacji: techniki definiowania problemu. *Ekonomiczne Problemy Usług, 122,* 269–278.

Khan, F. (2018). *Understanding the impact of technology in audit and finance.* London: The Institute of Chartered Accountants in England and Wales, The Dubai Financial Services Authority.

Kisperska-Moroń, D., & Krzyżaniak, S. (2009). *Logistyka.* Poznań: Wydawnictwo ILIM.

Klein, S. (2018). *Logistics audit identifying fields of action to optimize service, quality and costs.* Frankfurt am Main: Miebach Consulting White Paper.

Klug, F. (2018). *Logistikmanagement in Automobilindustrie. Grundlagen der Logistik im Automobilbau.* Berlin: Springer.

Kotler, P., et al. (2010). *Marketing management.* New York: Prentice Hall.

Kowalczyk, L. (2015). Logistics supply as an element of logistic infrastructure in gastronomy on selected example. *Journal of Translogistics.* Wrocław, 139–155.

Kozina, A. (2014). Coalition strategy in (multiparty) negotiations. *Zeszyty Naukowe Uniwersytetu Ekonomiczno-Przyrodniczego w Siedlcach, Seria: Administracja i Zarządzanie, 100,* 67–82.

Krawczyk, S. (2000). *Logistyka w zarządzaniu marketingiem.* Wrocław: Wydawnictwo Akademii Ekonomicznej.

Krzyżaniak, S., Niemczyk, A., Majewski, J., & Andrzejczyk, P. (2014). *Organizacja i monitorowanie procesów magazynowych* (2nd ed.). Poznań: Instytut Logistyki i Magazynowania (ILiM).

Krzyżanowski, L. (1994). *Podstawy nauk o organizacji i zarządzaniu* (2nd ed.). Warszawa: Wydawnictwo Naukowe PWN.

Kulińska, E., & Koziarska, A. (2017). Significance and impact of outsourcing of logistics processes – Case study. *Econometrics, 1*(55). The Univeristy of Technology in Opole. https://doi.org/10.15611/ekt.2017.1.07.

Kupisiewicz, Cz. (1964). *O efektívnosti problémového vyučovania.* Bratislava: SPN.

Lancioni, R. (1991). Distribution cost accounting in international logistics. *International Journal of Physical Distribution and Logistics Management, 21*(8), 12–16.

Langley, G. J., Nolan, K. M., Nolan, T. W., Norman, C. L., & Provost, L. P. (1996). *The improvement guide.* San Francisco: Jossey-Bass Publishers.

Larina, P. P. (2005). *Logistics: Textbook.* Donetsk: Era.

Lee, J., Bagheri, B., Kao, H. A., & Lapira, E. (2015). Industry 4.0 and manufacturing transformation. *Manufacturing Leadership Journal, Vol. 4.*

Linhart, J. (1976). *Činnost a poznávání.* Praha: Academia.

Lisiński, M. (2011). *Audyt wewnętrzny w doskonaleniu instytucji.* Warszawa: Polskie Wydawnictwo Ekonomiczne.

Łobejko, S. (2018). *Strategie cyfryzacji przedsiębiorstw,* t. 2, Materiały konferencyjne, XXI Konferencja Innowacje w Zarządzaniu i Inżynierii, Polskie Towarzystwo Zarządzania Produkcją, Zakopane.

Lwowski, B., & Kozłowski, R. (2007). *Podstawowe zagadnienia zarządzania produkcją.* Kraków: Oficyna Ekonomiczna.

136   References

Lysons, K. (2004). *Zakupy zaopatrzeniowe*. Warszawa: Polskie Wydawnictwo Ekonomiczne.

Malindžák, D., Kačmáry, P., Ostasz, G., Gazda, A., Zatwarnicka-Madura, B., & Lorek, M. (2015). *Design of logistic systems. Theory and applications*. New York: Open Science Publishers.

Mastalerz-Kodzis, A. (2018). Methodology of the measurement of territorial unit and organization economical potencial. *Scientific Papers of Silesian University of Technology, Organization and Management Series, 127*, 125–134.

Mazzone, D. M. (2014). *Digital or death: Digital transformation: The only choice for business to survive smash and conquer*. Smashbox Consulting Inc, Ontario.

Merchant, K. A. (1985). *Control in business organizations*. Boston: Pitman.

Meuldijk, M. (2017). Impact of digitization on the audit profession. *Audit Committee News*, Edition 58, Q3 2017, KPMG AG.

Młodzik, E. (2013). Identyfikacja ryzyka – kluczowy element procesu zarządzania ryzykiem w jednostkach gospodarczych. *Zeszyty Naukowe Uniwersytetu Szczecińskiego, 61*, Wydawnictwo Uniwersytetu Szczecińskiego, Szczecin.

Montgomery, R. H. (1956). *Dicksee's auditing. CPA handbook*. Durham: American Institute of Certified Public Accountants.

Mroczko, F. (2016). *Logistyka*. Prace Naukowe Wyższej Szkoły Zarządzania i Przedsiębiorczości. Seria: Zarządzanie, 46. Wałbrzych.

Mynarski, S. (1979). *Elementy teorii systemów i cybernetyki*. Warszawa: Państwowe Wydawnictwo Naukowe.

Nassab, S. G. H. H., Shenass, M. R. K., Aramesh, P., & Nasab, S. M. H. (2013). The effect of production management on increase productivity operations management of Shahid Hashemi Nejad Gas Refinery (Khangiran). *European Online Journal of Natural and Social Sciences, 2*(3), Special Issue on Accounting and Management, 2827–2838.

Nasta, L. N., & Ladar, C. T. (2015). Convergences and divergences between internal and external audit on international context. *AGORA International Journal of Administration Sciences, 1*, 46–55.

Nogalski, B., & Marcinkiewicz, H. (2004). *Zarządzanie antykryzysowe przedsiębiorstwem. Pokonać kryzys i wygrać*. Warszawa: Difin.

Norman, M. (2009). *A look into the future: The next evolution of internal audit continuous risk and control assurance*. Germany: SAP AG.

Nosal, Cz. (1993). *Umysł menedżera*. Wrocław: Wrocławskie Wydawnictwo Przecinek.

Nowakowska, A. (2019). Managing distribution processes in the selected sales. *Network World Scientific News, 123*, 234–245.

Nowicka-Skowron, M. (2000). *Efektywność systemów logistycznych*. Warszawa: Polskie Wydawnictwo Ekonomiczne.

Oklander, M. A. (2005). *Logistics: Textbook*. Kiev: Foreign Trade.

Pająk, W. (2008). Audyt organizacji systemu logistycznego przedsiębiorstwa w procesie tworzenia zintegrowanego łańcucha dostaw. *Zeszyty Naukowe, 774*, 69–83.

Penc, J. (2007). *Leksykon biznesu*. Warszawa: Agencja Wydawnicza Placet.

Petrascu, D. (2010). Internal audit: Defining, objectives, functions and stages. *Studies in Business and Economics, 5*(3). Lucian Blaga University of Sibiu, Faculty of Economic Sciences, 238–246 .

Pfohl, H. Ch. (1998). *Zarządzanie logistyką.* Poznań: ILiM.

Pienaar, W. (2009). *Introduction to business logistics.* Cape Town: Oxford University.

Pieriegud, J. (2016). Cyfryzacja gospodarki i społeczeństwa – wymiar globalny, europejski i krajowy. In J. Gajewski, W. Paprocki & J. Pieriegud (Eds.), *Cyfryzacja gospodarki i społeczeństwa. Szanse i wyzwania dla sektorów infrastrukturalnych* (pp. 11–13). Gdańsk: Instytut Badań nad Gospodarką Rynkową – Gdańska Akademia Bankowa.

Pop, A., Bota-Avram, C., & Bota-Avram, F. (2008). The relationship between internal and external audit. *Annales Universitatis Apulensis Series Oeconomica, 1*(10), 18.

PwC. (2019). *Transport Przyszłości. Raport o perspektywach rozwoju transportu drogowego w Polsce w latach 2020–2030.* Warszawa, PWC project.

Razik, M., Radi, B., & Okar, Ch. (2017). Development of a maturity model for the warehousing function in Moroccan companies. *International Journal of Engineering and Technology (IJET), 9*(2), 280–290. https://doi.org/10.21817/ijet/2017/v9i1/170902303.

Roland Berger Strategy Consultants GmbH. (2015). *The digital transformation of industry. How important is it? Who are the winners? What must be done now?* München, Germany.

RSM International Association. (2019). *Internal audit – The changing landscape.* Mumbai, India: RSM Astute Consulting Pvt. Ltd.

Rut, J., & Miłasiewicz, B. (2016). Logistyka procesu magazynowania w wybranym przedsiębiorstwie – studium przypadku. *Gospodarka Materiałowa i Logistyka, 9,* 24–30.

Satka, E. (2017). Internal and external audit in the function of the management of the trade companies. *Journal of US–China Public Administration, 14*(6), 330–338. https://doi.org/10.17265/1548–6591/2017.06.004.

Savić, D. (2019). From cigitization, through digitalization, to digital transformation. January/February, *Online Searcher*, 36–39.

Sawyer, B. L., Dittenhofer, A. M., & Scheiner, H. J. (2003). *Sawyer's internal auditing. 5th edition. The practice of modern internal auditing.* Altamonte Springs, FL: The Institute of Internal Auditors.

Skrzypek, A. (2014). Qualitative aspects of the improvement of the organization's management. *Zeszyty Naukowe Uniwersytetu Przyrodniczo-Humanistycznego w Siedlcach, Seria: Administracja i Zarządzanie, 100,* 131–146.

Skuza, Z. (2019). Selected aspects of supply logistics in the analyzed enterprise. *Gospodarka Materiałowa i Logistyka, 11,* t. LXXI. https://doi.org/10.33226/1231-2037.2019.11.1.

Śledziewska, K., & Włoch, R. (2020). *Gospodarka cyfrowa. Jak nowe technologie zmieniają świat.* Warszawa: Wydawnictwa Uniwersytetu Warszawskiego.

Śliżewska, J., & Zadrożna, D. (2014). *Organizowanie i monitorowanie dystrybucji Kwalifikacja A.30.2.* Warszawa: Wydawnictwa Szkolne i Pedagogiczne.

Sljivic, S., Skorup, S., & Vukadinovic, P. (2015). Management control in modern organizations. *International Review, 3–4.* https://doi.org/10.5937/intrev1504039S.

Słowiński, B. (2008). *Wprowadzenie do logistyki*. Koszalin: Wydawnictwo Uczelniane Politechniki Koszalińskiej.

Statistics Poland. (2020). *Materials management in 2019. Statistical analyses*. Warsaw, November, Warsaw, Poland.

Sungurtekin, T. (2011). *How a logistics audit can identify bottlenecks and improvements for organizations*. Retrieved from http://EzineArticles.com/.

Swinkels, W. H. A. (2012). *Exploration of a theory of internal audit: A study on the theoretical foundations of internal audit in relation to the nature and the control systems of Dutch public listed firms*. Delft: Eburon.

Szczepańska, K. (2011). *Zarządzanie jakością. W dążeniu do doskonałości*. Warszawa: Wydawnictwo C.H. Beck.

Szklarski, L., & Kozioł, R. (1980). *Systemy sterowania procesem technologicznym w górnictwie*. Warszawa–Kraków: Państwowe Wydawnictwo Naukowe.

Szymonik, A. (2014). Ryzyko w systemach logistycznych. *Zeszyty Naukowe Politechniki Łódzkiej, Seria: Organizacja i Zarządzanie, 1193*, z 58.

Tannenbaum, A. S. (1962). Control in organizations: Individual adjustment and organizational performance. *Administrative Science Quarterly, 7*(2), 236–257.

Tapscott, D. (1998). *Gospodarka cyfrowa. Nadzieje i niepokoje Ery Świadomości Systemowej*. Warszawa: Business Press.

Testa, M. R., & Sipe, J. L. (2013). The organizational culture audit: Countering cultural ambiguity in the service context. *Open Journal of Leadership, 2*(2), 36–44. https://doi.org/10.4236/ojl.2013.22005.

The Institute of Internal Auditors. (2016). *All in day's work a look at the varied responsibilities of internal auditors*, No. 10. United States: Global Headquarters.

Trenkner, M. (2016). Doskonalenie procesów i ich uwarunkowania. *Journal of Management and Finance, 14*(2–1), 429–438.

Twaróg, J. (2003). *Mierniki i wskaźniki logistyczne*. Poznań: ILiM.

Voortman, C. (2004). *Global logistics management*. Cape Town: Juta and Co Ltd.

Wąchol, J. (2010). Nowoczesne instrumenty zarządzania a nadzór korporacyjny. *Zeszyty Naukowe Uniwersytetu Szczecińskiego. Studia Informatica, 26*, 155–165.

Wasiak, M. (2013). Uwarunkowania stosowania systemu logistycznego do optymalizacji potencjałów systemów przewozowych. *Logistyka, 4*, 757–768.

Wawrzynowicz, J., & Wajszczuk, K. (2012). *The model of logistics audit for agricultural enterprises*. In Proceedings of the Carpathian Logistics Congress, 7–9 November. Jesenik: Czech Republic.

Żebrucki, Z. (2012). Rola audytu w usprawnianiu systemu logistycznego przedsiębiorstwa. Zeszyty Naukowe Politechniki Śląskiej: Organizacja i Zarządzanie, vol. 60, pp. 421–433.

Ziyadin, S., Suieubayeva, S., & Utegenova, A. (2020). Digital transformation in business. In S. Ashmarina, M. Vochozka & V. Mantulenko (Eds.), *Digital age: Chances, challenges and future. ISCDTE 2019*. Lecture Notes in Networks and

Systems, vol 84. Cham: Springer. https://doi.org/10.1007/978-3-030-27015-5
_49.

Žofková, M., & Drábek, J. (2019). *Application of innovative approaches in enterprise management based on the logistic audit.* 11th International Scientific Conference Economics, Management and Technology in Enterprises 2019 (EMT 2019). Advances in Economics, Business and Management Research, 78.ww

Index

Note: Page locators in italics refer to figures and bold refer to tables.

For Product Safety Concerns and Information please contact our EU
representative GPSR@taylorandfrancis.com
Taylor & Francis Verlag GmbH, Kaufingerstraße 24, 80331 München, Germany

www.ingramcontent.com/pod-product-compliance
Lightning Source LLC
Chambersburg PA
CBHW061323220326
41599CB00026B/5009